Charles Topper, EdD

Spirituality in Pastoral Counseling and the Community Helping Professions

More pre-publication
REVIEWS, COMMENTARIES, EVALUATIONS . . .

"**W**ith the clarity and expertise that can come only from years of personal experience as a counselor, Charles Topper shows that knowing how to integrate spirituality and spiritual issues in the counseling setting is not only practical but profoundly important for all in the helping professions today."

Louis M. Savary, PhD, STD
Author, *Kything:*
The Art of Spiritual Presence

The Haworth Pastoral Press®
An Imprint of The Haworth Press, Inc.
New York • London • Oxford

Spirituality
in Pastoral Counseling
and the Community
Helping Professions

THE HAWORTH PASTORAL PRESS
Religion and Mental Health
Harold G. Koenig, MD
Senior Editor

Spirituality
in Pastoral Counseling
and the Community
Helping Professions

Charles Topper, EdD

The Haworth Pastoral Press®
An Imprint of The Haworth Press, Inc.
New York • London • Oxford

Published by

The Haworth Pastoral Press®, an imprint of The Haworth Press, Inc., 10 Alice Street, Binghamton, NY 13904-1580.

TR: 7.14.05

Cover design concept by Mary Livingstone.

Cover design by Jennifer M. Gaska.

Library of Congress Cataloging-in-Publication Data

Topper, Charles.
    Spirituality in pastoral counseling and the community helping professions / Charles Topper.
        p. cm.
Includes bibliographical references and index.
    ISBN 0-7890-0861-0 (alk. paper) — ISBN 0-7890-1848-9 (pbk. : alk. paper)
    1. Pastoral counseling. 2. Pastoral care. 3. Spirituality. I. Title.
BV4012.3.T67 2003
253.5—dc21
                                                        2002012077

To my past and present students
in pastoral ministry and pastoral counseling,
with gratitude for sharing your
experiences, questions, and ideas.

We have learned together.

ABOUT THE AUTHOR

Charles J. Topper, EdD, is Associate Professor of Counseling at St. Joseph College in West Hartford, Connecticut, where he teaches and supervises students in pastoral counseling and spiritual care. He is a licensed professional counselor, an approved clinical supervisor of the National Board for Certified Counselors, a certified chaplain of the National Association of Catholic Chaplains, and a counseling educator in the American Association of Pastoral Counseling. Dr. Topper is a priest from the Roman Catholic Diocese of Harrisburg, Pennsylvania. His professional interests and research are in the area of spirituality, spiritual care, and spiritual assessment in relation to counselor education and ministerial training. His work focuses on the development of a shared spiritual language for psychological and religious professionals. Dr. Topper has published articles in the *Journal of Pastoral Counseling, Vision,* and *Chicago Studies.*

CONTENTS

Preface

Spirituality in Pastoral Counseling and the Community Helping Professions presents a perspective and a vision. This perspective and vision articulates a clear rationale and strategies that helping professionals, religious and secular, can use to integrate spirituality into the practice of their caring work. This book began as a strong desire of many helping professionals, from hospice workers to social workers, to move spirituality more to the foreground in their work. A psychologist, Paul Pruyser, began a movement back in the 1960s and 1970s. He called upon religious professionals to draw more extensively upon their religious and spiritual resources in working with their patients. Through working with hospital chaplains, he discovered that more often than not they functioned more as counselors than as chaplains. True, religious professionals needed to use psychological counseling skills to develop a helping relationship and to facilitate emotional healing. However, in his work, *The Minister As Diagnostician* (1976), Pruyser challenged and encouraged these same spiritual caregivers to return more to the healing energies of their own field's religious and spiritual frameworks. As one author explains it, a chaplain needs to be more a shepherd than a psychotherapist (Clinebell, 1984).

A frequent complaint of students training in clinical pastoral education programs has been that their preparation is mostly psychological, and that a stronger focus on spirituality is needed. How does the chaplain use the patient's spirituality and theological beliefs in a helping relationship? Traditionally pastoral counselors have seen themselves as psychological counselors who are also available to work with problems as they relate to religion and ultimate values. Now, graduates of pastoral counseling masters' programs go further than did traditional pastoral counselors (Giblin and Stark-Dykema, 1992). They intentionally aim to *actively* integrate spirituality and theology into psychological helping. More and more, they are developing a psychospiritual approach to helping and healing. For them, pastoral counseling is not just counseling related to religion and ultimate values. Rather, pastoral counseling is psychological counseling that regularly uses the helpee's spirituality for support and problem clarification. This use of spirituality in counseling can alleviate client distress and facilitate personal adjustment.

Many in secular helping professions, especially nurses, counselors, and medical doctors, have expressed a strong desire to integrate spirituality into their helping work. To begin this work, they needed to develop a method of spiritual assessment. Nursing was the first of these three professions to develop ways to identify and work with patients' spirituality. True, the chaplain works with a person's religious and spiritual needs and the doctor with physical and medical needs. However, just as nurses meet the daily medical needs of the patient in conjunction with the doctor, many also see themselves in conjunction with the chaplain—attending to the spiritual needs of their patients. Nurses, as a result of this practice and their research, now have a well-developed process of spiritual assessment (Carpenito, 1997).

With regard to counselors, the Center for the Accreditation of Counseling and Related Education Programs (CACREP) notes that counselors need to develop specific competencies in the area of spirituality (Burke, 2000). Spirituality is viewed as an integral part of human growth and development. Counselors need to be able to work with it. For example, CACREP speaks of a counselor's needed competency "to assess the relevance of spirituality in the client's therapeutic issues" (p. 2). Counselors realize that they are not only agents of behavioral change but, through working with clients' spirituality, they can also become instruments of internal healing. It is one thing to work with a client's problems, but another thing to find internal peace in the process.

Finally, in the practice of the medical profession itself, there is a strong movement focusing on the importance of spirituality and religion in mental and physical health (Koenig, 1997). Many research studies show religion and spirituality's role in human well-being. From this ever-broadening search for spirituality led by nurses, hospital chaplains, pastoral and secular counselors, and medical doctors, we can clearly discern a deepening level of spiritual consciousness in all the caring professions. They are focusing more on the whole person—body, mind, and spirit. This book aims to assist these helping professionals, whether religious or secular, to work with their clients' spirituality.

My first hope is that religious/pastoral caregivers will develop stronger identities and spiritual care competencies in their pastoral work. Their seminary or ministry education rightly focused on theology, the study of the divine. Now, there is also a strong need to focus on the "clinical science of the spiritual dimension of the person" (McSherry, 1987, p. 3). At times, it appears that the religious professional comes across as too preachy or too dogmatic or too ritually focused. Or the religious professional downplays religion to appear more human and as a result comes across as a counselor or a psychologist. Facilitating a stronger spirituality into their theology, belief, and ritual will show a more appealing way for these professionals. This book will accomplish this goal by showing helpers ways to facilitate reflection on spiritual needs. These spiritual needs can then be related to helpees' religious or spiritual traditions. In this process, I also wish to help ritual religious caregivers identify and reach the deeper spiritual focus of their work. Through the repeated use of the same signs and symbols, they may frequently feel frustration, evaluating themselves as simply pastoral care functionaries. This book will help these spiritual caregivers to develop a deeper sense of spiritual needs in the midst of their healing ritual work. Spirituality and competent spiritual care will strengthen and enrich the identities of these religious leaders as professional caregivers (McSherry, 1987).

My second hope is to help counselors and other community helping professionals integrate spirituality into their practice through the development of a broader spiritual vision of the human person. These helping professionals may experience discomfort with this prospect, fearing that they are moving into a field that is not of their competence. After all, they are not religious professionals. However, spirituality lives within the person. It is a part of everyone's psyche. As such, it is part of clinical practice. Indeed many counselors and psychologists now realize that their work is not complete until their clients examine their problems in the context of the deeper meanings and connections of their lives. Psychological professionals see an expanded need for spirituality particularly with client problems centered on loss. This book will show them how to use their clients' spirituality and spiritual needs in this process. Most important, in this regard, secular helping professionals and indeed religious professionals need to develop a broader vocabulary of spirituality to identify and work practically with clients' spiritual needs. Developing a standard vocabulary to use in spirituality will professionally show the vitality of this area for human growth and development.

My third hope is that this book will be a useful resource in the helping fields of ministry education, psychological training, and human development. A focus on spirituality will bring a stronger identity to these fields of study and service. My hope is that teachers, ministers, learners, trainers, supervisors, and supervisees will use this book as a resource to make spirituality and spiritual care a key focus of their education and training. I certainly do not want to replace or downplay the primary importance of the helping relationship and psychological care. We know that healthy spiritual care takes place only in conjunction with a sound helping relationship. However, most texts in the helping fields have either ignored spirituality or at the most viewed spiritual care as an addendum to helping and psychological care. Spirituality has been thin icing on a piece of cake, rather than a hefty piece of bread that holds life together. The time has come for a book whose primary purpose is spirituality and spiritual care counseling for the community helping professions.

Although this book does not offer a new theory of spirituality or pastoral care, it does follow a particular perspective. I have purposely chosen the words "spiritual care" rather than "pastoral care." *I see spiritual care as assisting the person in her or his spiritual needs leading to spiritual well-being. I see pastoral care as spiritual care carried out using the resources of a particular faith or religious tradition.* In essence, spiritual care is broader than pastoral care in that it can be carried out either within a religious tradition or within a secular helping environment as we shall further examine in Chapter 1. Spirituality is the core or integrating principle either of a person's religious beliefs or of another viewpoint of life. Spirituality and spiritual care are essential parts of both effective pastoral care and holistic psychological care. Indeed, it is the affirmation of this book that both religious pastoral care and psychological care are integrated and find completion in nourishing spiritual care. Enabling all helpers, religious and secular, to have more confidence and competencies in working with spirituality is the goal of this book.

My fourth hope is that the stronger integration of spirituality into psychology and religion will bring them closer together. First, with the age of science and the enlightenment, and second and more recently, with Freudian psychoanalysis, psychology and religion have been split. Spirituality can, however, now become a common meeting point and a connecting link between secular helping professionals and pastoral care leaders. Moreover, the common focus on spirituality can draw diverse religions closer together. The dogmas may differ, but the spiritual needs beneath them are one. Religions with one another and psychology with religion share a common human spirituality.

This book expects to expand the horizons of spirituality for both pastoral counselors and other helping professions. This will be done not so much by original research as by bringing together and building upon the results of research and practices by nurses, counselors, and chaplains over the last three decades. First, we will accomplish our goal by looking at the phenomenon of spirituality: what is it; what is its core; what makes care spiritual? After all, a helper may say that she or he is spiritual but not recognize spiritual needs, nor provide a method for spiritual development. Only when we clearly see what spirituality is and identify spiritual needs in the person will we begin to see spiritual care's ever-expanding horizons. At that point, we will see wider possibilities for future spiritual care and identify more clearly spirituality in our own present work.

Second, we will expand the horizons of spiritual care by developing a method of assessing spiritual needs and working with a person's spirituality. This method will create a more intentional and hence more active practice of spirituality. It will assist those in secular and religious helping positions to respond more effectively to their clients' and members' spiritual needs. It will help make the traditionally intuitive process of pastoral care more open.

Third, we will expand the horizons of spiritual care by sharing some instruments of spiritual assessment useful in various care settings. This is a beginning but growing area. Professional helping organizations are looking for an instrument to help others and to document their work in spiritual care.

Fourth, we will expand the horizons of spiritual care by developing a list of competencies that are needed to be an effective spiritual caregiver whether in pastoral care or other community helping. What skills are actually involved in effective spiritual care? We will also include a section on spiritual care standards for organizations involved in whole person care. Through expanding their horizons of spirituality and spiritual care, secular and religious helpers and their organizations will see the healing effects of spirituality in people's lives. They will wondrously experience their roles as helpers focused more on spiritual growth. The counselor will remain a counselor; the psychologist a psychologist; the religious professional will remain religious. However, through the integration of spirituality more fully into psychology and into religion, the helpee's psyche and soul will better meet and even come together. The whole person, body, mind, and *spirit* will be served.

Chapter 1, "Spirituality: A Growing Focus for Professional Caregivers," will guide the reader to examine and to reflect on just what spirituality is in regard to spiritual care. It will explore various descriptions of spirituality in order to develop an understanding of what human spiritual needs are. The reader will learn the distinctions and similarities between religion and spirituality. How might the helper use them separately or together depending on the particular client? Moreover, how do spiritual needs relate to a person's psychological and possible religious needs? Are they similar, very separate, closely related? Are spiritual needs really psychological needs using a different terminology or are spiritual needs distinct from psychological needs? As readers answer these questions, they will expand their vocabulary of spirituality and spiritual needs. They will develop competency in identifying, naming, and working with spiritual needs in self and others. Finally in this chapter, readers will learn how to identify helpees in times of "spiritual distress" and help them return to and grow in "spiritual well-being."

Chapter 2, "Spiritual Assessment," presents a practical, clear, and simple model of spiritual assessment. It is a model that caregivers can regularly and easily work with to identify the spiritual needs of helpees. It includes a process of assessing spiritual needs through a listening conversation with the helpee. The helper listens to the helpee's story in order to identify spiritual needs in the helpee's life. This chapter views spiritual assessment holistically as a willfully intentional practice useful for both the psychological and religious professional.

Chapter 3, "The Process of Spiritual Care," first places the process of spiritual assessment within the broader context of the kind of care a helpee needs whether social, psychological, spiritual, or ritual. Second, it expands spiritual assessment into a larger process of spiritual care. Practically speaking, what is the goal of spiritual care? Is it mainly to sustain the helpee in a very difficult situation? Is it to offer guidance in a complicated problem? Or is it to facilitate healing within the self and/or reconciliation with others? Third, in this chapter the helper will learn when applicable how to assess and utilize the helpee's beliefs and/or religious needs in the spiritual care and growth process.

The purpose of the models of spiritual assessment and care in Chapters 2 and 3 is not to categorize and diagnose the person, as is frequently done in psychological assessment. Nor is it to take the role of the confessor in religious assessment. Rather, their purpose is to give both the helper and the helpee an awareness of spiritual needs, perspectives, and goals in order to lead the person to human integration and spiritual growth. Spiritual assessment and care are simply sensible ways to make concrete the spiritual needs that each of us has. The purpose of Chapters 2 and 3 is to bring practical methods or tools to the surface to work with helpees' spirituality and spiritual needs. We live in an age of accountability and evaluation. Do we really do what we say when we call ourselves spiritual caregivers or holistic counselors? These models are an attempt to show that we can do this practically.

Chapter 4, "Tools for Spiritual Assessment: Spiritual Care As a Clinical Science," examines already-developed structured formal instruments of spiritual assessment. These clinical instruments assess a person's spiritual well-being, spiritual health, and even spiritual/religious experience. As seen in Chapter 2, an informal spiritual assessment carried out through a listening conversation is usually enough. However, employing a spiritual assessment instrument can make spirituality more concrete and real for the helpee. Also, an instrument can surface possible areas of spiritual exploration to be used later by the helper. Chapter 4 presents three formal spiritual assessment instruments to accomplish this. In addition, the reader will also become familiar with three developmental models of spiritual assessment that will explain how to assess spiritual needs across a person's life span. Following this, the reader will learn how to use a clinical instrument or developmental model as part of an interview process. This method is usually called a "semistructured interview" because it makes use of a personal interview with some structured questions or a formal spiritual assessment instrument. Having looked at clinical instruments and developmental models in the context of a semistructured interview, the reader will then be ready to think about developing his or her own survey or brief instrument of spiritual assessment. As part of this process, the reader will learn some guidelines and a useful structure for developing a spiritual assessment survey for his or her work and organization. Many helping and health care organizations are looking for such a survey to use with their clients in order to give their organization more accountability in the area of spirituality.

Chapters 5 and 6, "Basic Aptitudes and Skills of Spiritual Care" and "Broader Skills of Spiritual Care," look at individual competencies needed to do spiritual assessment and care. These chapters provide readers and practitioners with guidelines, principles, and standards to measure themselves against. In reality, these standards are also goals to reach and grow toward. As a person needs competencies to work with the psyche, so also with the spirit. Indeed, holistic helping professionals need competencies in both areas. Spiritual care thrives in an effective human helping relationship. Obviously, before the helper can do any spiritual care, he or she needs to be psychologically able to develop a helping relationship with helpees. If the helper does not relate to the helpee, little or no spiritual care takes place. When connected with the helpee, the helper then needs the ability to surface in the helpee a spiritual awareness related to his or her concerns. In this regard, can the helper facilitate the helpee spiritually in naming what is happening to him or her? For example, can the helper facilitate the helpee in naming a spiritual need for some meaning or hope in his or her difficult situation? The helper needs to be committed to the integration of spirituality in the person; and in this process, the helper needs to accept his or her identity as a spiritual caregiver. Moreover, in working with the helpee's spirituality, the helper will also need the psychological abilities to feel pain, loss, and grief with the helpee, and to relate the meaning of these to the ethnic or cultural background of the helpee. Ethnic background is particularly important in working with the helpee's image of God or a Higher Power. With a religious helpee, the helper needs competency in utilizing the helpee's beliefs and religious resources to facilitate needed personal healing. The competent spiritual caregiver values the "transformative wisdom of diverse religions and cultures" ("Report," 2001, p. 6).

Chapter 7, "A Community Model of Spiritual Care," presents a model that moves spiritual care beyond individual care alone into the community. This final chapter moves our focus of spiritual care from the individual to the organization. We will look at group standards of spiritual care. Spiritual care is not only individual care but also care for systems, organizations, and communities that facilitate spirituality. Increasingly organizations, especially health care groups, are asking for models or standards to determine the quality of spiritual care in their facilities. This concluding section will present a model that will effectively indicate standards of spiritual care useful for many organizations. Moreover, the spiritual caregiver as a helper who seeks to move beyond self and develop wider and deeper connections with the surrounding community needs the ability to live a social justice focus of spirituality and spiritual care. The spiritual caregiver "advocates for attention to the disenfranchised" ("Report," 2001, p. 6). Everyone's spirit and spirituality are deeply affected by the environments they work and live in.

After reading this book, individuals should have the confidence to be and do the following:

- Become more aware of spirituality and spiritual needs
- Not hesitate to work more with a client's spirituality
- Be able to think about and assess themselves and their clients from a spiritual perspective and not just from a psychological point of view
- Identify, learn, and effectively use a method of spiritual assessment and care
- Accept their identity as a spiritual caregiver
- Relate spiritual care to a helpee's ethnic heritage and how it influences him or her spiritually and indeed psychologically
- Effectively introduce them to some clinical instruments of spiritual assessment
- Teach them how to develop a spiritual assessment survey for their work setting
- Assess their own skills for and develop further competencies for spiritual care
- Establish standards of spiritual care for their own caregiving practice and that of the organization they serve

Acknowledgments

My gratitude goes out to many for this book. We discover our spirituality in our deepest connections beyond ourselves. A book such as this draws from the work, energy, and connection with many people, past and present, in the field. As the New World comes alive through deeper spiritual consciousness, we recognize our interdependence more and more. No one preparing a book in the area of spirituality ever works alone. We stand on the work of others. We plant some new seeds and cultivate further growth. Ultimately, we realize our deepest connection with the Divine, who works through us all.

My thanks to several pastoral counseling students who thoroughly proofread and gave valuable feedback for part of this book: Linda Catrambone, Dennis Gallant, Stella Kouvakos, Pamela Lizdas Stack, and Joanne Wholey. I also wish to thank many students over years of teaching whose challenging questions, research, and writing have contributed to this work, especially Rick Pacukonas, Jennifer Cimmino, Sr. Loretta Walsh, and Joanne Wholey. I am most grateful for the semester sabbatical spent in research at Union Theological Seminary in New York City, and for the research support of my librarian colleagues at St. Joseph College in West Hartford, Connecticut. Ms. Patricia Senich and help from the college's information technology department proved invaluable. Thanks and more thanks.

Over the years I have been continually grateful for my deceased colleague, Dr. Nancy Lund, for encouraging me to develop courses and to do research in the areas of spirituality and spiritual care. I also wish to thank Dr. Larry VandeCreek for facilitating and encouraging me to begin this project. Many spiritual care researchers and practitioners past and present have greatly influenced the development of this book. Among them are S. D. Arnold, A. Bergin, M. Burke, D. Capps, C. Cason, H. Clinebell, C. Ellison, G. Fitchett, D. Helminiak, M. Highfield, S. Ivy, E. Kelly, H. Koenig, H. N. Malony, E. McSherry, R. Nash, W. Oates, R. Paloutzian, J. Patton, P. Pruyser, P. S. Richards, D. Sappinton, and R. Stoll. The meaning of my life and life's work has grown through connectedness with these influential leaders in spirituality research and care.

Chapter 1

Spirituality: A Growing Focus for Professional Caregivers

WHAT IS SPIRITUALITY?

What is spirituality? When I hear the word, the phrase "spiritual life" comes to mind. From my Catholic Christian tradition, spirituality immediately causes me to reflect on my prayer life and my relationship with God. As I hear the word, I ask myself, "What is presently happening in my prayer life? Am I taking time to be with Christ? Is my spiritual life progressing?" For me, spirituality is equated with spiritual formation. For others, it may bring a much different feeling and picture. Indeed, there are probably as many reactions and descriptions of spirituality as there are people. Perhaps we should use the plural "spiritualities." Regardless, spirituality is a word weighted with multiple contemporary meanings. "It is a term whose meaning is at once evident and elusive . . . referring to many aspects of a person's or group's way of being" (Thayer, 1985, p. 31).

The following examples illustrate this multiplicity and diversity:

- A Christian-sponsored hospital advertises itself as a center of "spirituality and healing" for the new millennium.
- The news media frequently runs short segments on the relationship of spirituality to good health.
- Individuals forcefully pointing out that they are spiritual but not religious. A CNN/USA Today Gallup Poll (Moore and Saad, 1999) shows that 30 percent of Americans view themselves in this way.
- Religious organizations, through their scriptures and practices, present themselves as the key centers for spiritual growth and development in this world; yet even people in secular helping

professions call themselves "spiritual healers" and practice as such.

- Some psychological counselors speak of treating the whole person through body, mind, and spirit, thus working with the spiritual nature or spirituality of their clients.
- Spiritual directors speak of spirituality more explicitly as one's active response to God acting in one's life. They speak of a lived spirituality and follow a particular school of spirituality such as Lutheran, which emphasizes grace, salvation, and forgiveness, or Franciscan spirituality, which focuses on following Christ through a life of simplicity and even poverty.
- Many departments of pastoral care in health care institutions have changed their titles to departments of spiritual care.
- Nurses, chaplains, pastoral counselors, and others speak of compiling a spiritual assessment of their patients and working with their religions or spirituality as part of a health care plan.
- Many helping professionals fear that spirituality has become too intellectual. They view it as an experience or feeling of peace and deeper connection in life to self, others, and a Higher Power.
- Some areas of contemporary physical science speak of spirituality as part of one's human nature, not a supernatural addition to one's humanity (see Helminiak, 1996).

The term *spirituality* is used so widely today that we frequently have to stop and reflect on its meaning. However, this multiplicity does show that many different groups have finally accepted spirituality in the modern world. Wondrously, we have and are reversing the purely scientific focus of the past three centuries since the Age of Enlightenment. What is occurring is similar to what happened when people in congregations and churches began to speak of ministry in a wider perspective than simply that of the professional minister. Similarly, spirituality is now viewed more widely than simply the spirituality equated with church, God, or religion. In the thirteenth century the saint and philosopher Thomas Aquinas wrote of how one meets God through human rationality as well as through revealed faith. Today, the modern movement of spirituality reminds us that we can experience spirituality in human nature as well as through meeting God. Indeed, each person experiences spirituality throughout his or her life experiences, culture, and values.

What then is spirituality? Because of the great variety of explanations it is impossible to give one essential definition. Perhaps the best way to proceed is to give a short synopsis of various descriptions of spirituality from the previously described types of people. From them we can draw out the core elements that describe spirituality. Before we proceed, take a few moments and write down your own explanation of spirituality. What key points encompass spirituality for you? At the end of this section you will be able to determine whether your description contains the elements that others generally consider spirituality. You can agree or disagree.

Reflection Questions: What does spirituality encompass for you? To whom are you grateful for your sense of spirituality? Do you see your spirituality growing? (If you find it difficult to get in touch with your spirituality, slow down, relax, breathe deeply, and take some quiet time to reflect and get in touch with your inner self. Take a walk outside. Attend a religious service. Listen to and feel some beautiful and heartwarming music.)

Simply Human (Human Spiritual Dimension)

The following description of spirituality was developed at the 1971 White House Conference on Aging:

> We shall consider "the spiritual" as pertaining to man's [woman's] ~~Tillich~~ inner resources, especially his [her] ultimate concern, the basic value around which all other values are focused, the central philosophy of life . . . which guides a person's conduct, the supernatural and nonmaterial dimensions of human nature. We shall assume, therefore, that all men [women] are "spiritual," even if they . . . practice no personal pieties. (Moberg, 1971, p. 3)

This was one of the first times that helping professionals looked at spirituality apart from a God-centered or religious context. The helping professionals participating in this conference on aging saw spirituality wherever they encountered people's ultimate concerns or key values. This is why some people now describe themselves as spiritual but not religious. Their ultimate value may be a belief in bringing good into the world or a belief in personal growth without any religious faith. Consequently, our culture's key value or spirituality might be freedom, or it might well be prosperity with the belief in a better material life for its people. Abraham Maslow calls our material focus a "pseudo spirituality that is ultimately not fulfilling" (in Loury, 1979, p. 876). Nonetheless, even a material focus may be a particular person's or group's spirituality. What are the key focuses of your life? These might well be your spirituality.

The White House Conference's description sees all people as spiritual simply for being human or having a human nature. Spirituality is part of everyone's human nature. Every person has an inborn capacity to develop basic values and beliefs around which that person centers his or her life. As such, everyone shares a spiritual nature. Carl Jung (1959), referring to such a spiritual nature, goes so far as to claim that a spiritual function indeed is found in every human psyche with energy as powerful as any of our other instincts. As humans we are not just bodies with physical and psychological instincts. We are spiritual creatures with a strong spiritual instinct. Spirituality is not only a belief but a vital force (Lowen, 1990) within our bodies and minds. All of this leads us to an expanded conceptualization of human spirituality. Do you agree or disagree with spirituality as an innate construct or capacity found in every human being?

Reflection Questions: What are the key values of your life? Is it being yourself, close relationships with family and friends, a successful career, material possessions and wealth, a close relationship with God, a strong faith community, the freedom to make choices, serving others? What values do you incorporate into your life? Where do your spirit and spirituality reside?

Religious Spirituality (Religious Spiritual Dimension)

Although spirituality and religion are not necessarily similar, they overlap for most people. The following describes spirituality from a more specific religious point of view:

> The term spirituality, therefore, embraces everything that we are, think and do in relation to the triune God who is present in and yet transcends all that is. Spirituality might be defined as a style of life that flows from the presence of the Spirit within us and within the church, the Temple of the Holy Spirit. (McBrien, 1987, p. 79)

Religious spirituality focuses on spirituality within a theological context of belief in God and a religious context lived in a faith community. In this perspective, theology or religious experience comes first, and spirituality grows out of or builds upon theology and religious beliefs. It views spirituality less as part of our created human nature, and more as human nature's connection to God and the Divine. God, as such, is our ultimate connection or value. Hence our spirituality is God-focused. Donald Browning, a Christian theologian who writes on the relationship of psychology to religion, expands on the previous definition of spirituality by relating it even more to theology and the specific practices of religion:

> The term spirituality has a variety of meanings in the contemporary discussion but in general it refers to that dimension of Christian living that emphasizes various disciplines and practices designed to deepen one's sense of being related to the divine. (in Thayer, 1985, p. 7)

From these descriptions of spirituality, we can see how religious groups view it as a divine way of life growing out of religious beliefs. Spirituality is our response to God's action or grace in our lives rather than simply a part of our human nature. God acts first. We respond. Helminiak terms this feature of spirituality *"uncreated"* spirituality (p. 16) or a spirituality not created as part of our human nature but freely given to us as grace by God. For example, as a Christian, one ideally believes in God, Christ, and the Holy Spirit. Spirituality evolving from this relationship may be composed of a prayer life, participation in a Christian community, and service to the poor. Spirituality in this case is the practice of living in relationship with and participating in the grace of God. As Adrian Van Kaam (1975) states,

> Spirituality, therefore, in present day understanding, could be called the theoretical science of how to live the spiritual life. . . . Spirituality is not primarily a system of speculation about the "what" or the essence of the spiritual life; it is a theory about how practically to live the life of the spirit. (p. 37)

Reflection Questions: If you follow a religion, where does this spiritual path take you? What are the strengths or focuses of spirituality in your religious tradition?

In contrast to uncreated spirituality or grace, Helminiak uses the term *"created"* spirituality (1996, p. 16) not to describe religious practices but simply to describe an essential spiritual feature created in every person's human nature (see Figure 1.1). We can discover our spirituality in our own human connections within ourselves, with others, with the world around us, and beyond. One might see and feel spirituality in nature, in relationships with friends, in a chosen occupation; spirituality is not found only in scriptures and traditions. The first description of spirituality from the White House Conference on Aging agrees with this idea of a given created spirituality, thereby broadening the term *spirituality* beyond religious beliefs and practices. However, it is important to note that even in religion, our human or created spirituality would be the core of spirituality behind or beneath our religious spiritual practices and beliefs. A need to reach beyond the self to the divine arises from a spiritual need created deep within the self. In sum, spirituality is "the life principle that pervades a person's entire being, including volitional, emotional, moral-ethical, intellectual, and physical dimensions, and generates a capacity for transcendent values" (Colliton, 1981, p. 492).

Nurses are a good example of a group of helping professionals that works with a spirituality, beginning with created human nature. Facing the sickness, health, death, and life of their patients each day, nurses ask themselves, What is the life principle or meaning of life for this patient? What beyond self or deep within self will give this patient strength and courage in the midst of sickness and pain? Where does this patient's spirit reside? This is his or her spirituality—the natural spirituality or the spiritual base underneath the person's practice of spirituality or religion. Spirituality is not only a person's response to God's action in his or her life, but rather spirituality is the universal yearning for meaning and connection beyond self that everyone naturally has.

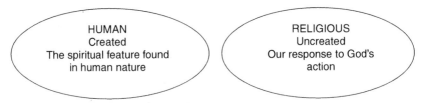

FIGURE 1.1. The Dual Nature of Spirituality

Based on these descriptions, spirituality (human and religious, created and uncreated) can be summarized as encompassing some or all of the following key elements:

1. A life principle created within us reaching every aspect of our existence—body, mind, and spirit
2. An experience or movement beyond and deep within reaching *trans. + immanent* for meaning and connection with the mystery of self, others, and the world
3. The ultimate concern and value that one strives to live and integrate *Tillich*
4. A connection with mystery and/or a Higher Power or God
5. An experience lived in a religious context responding to God's action or grace

I see numbers one, two, and three as encompassing human or created spirituality, and numbers four and five as usually religious or uncreated spirituality.

Where then do we find spirituality in our lives? Spirituality is involved when a friend reaches beyond self to connect with another friend, when a student searches for meaning, when a person in prayer seeks union with God, when a nurse or a counselor helps a client find hope, when a cleric leads prayer or celebrates a sacrament leading the congregation into deeper mystery, when anyone goes out of self to serve the world. All of these people enliven their own spirits and the human spirits of those whom they encounter. Any movement deep within the self or beyond the self toward a wider and fuller connection is part of the wondrous process of spirituality. The possibilities of spirituality and spiritual experience for the person are numerous, deep, and rich. They can never be finished.

With this broadened picture of both created and uncreated spirituality, we can further see that spirituality is a true unifying force for all humans regardless of ethnicity, background, or personal beliefs. A common thirst for the spiritual path can unite those having a religious spirituality with those who follow other spiritual paths. Spirituality is an inclusive term with an ecumenical universal force. All are spiritual who seek a life of meaning and purpose. As teachers, counselors, religious professionals, nurses, and numerous other helping professionals, let us all be more attuned to and celebrate the spirit and spirituality of ourselves and those for whom we care.

Reflection Questions: As a helper, what is the focus of your spirituality? What are the focuses of your helpees' spirituality? How do they look for meaning? What do they treasure? How do they celebrate their lives? What are their deepest connections within and beyond themselves? Do you agree that spirituality can be a unifying element among many diverse religions?

SPIRITUALITY AND HEALTHY RELIGION

In the past, religions might have too easily attempted to include all the parameters of spirituality within themselves. They have sometimes viewed organizations beyond themselves as secular or worldly. However, the opposite exists today when some people who are indeed spiritually focused exclude religion from spirituality. They may too easily equate religion only with dogma and ritual and not with strong possibilities of spiritual growth. They divide religion and spirituality. True, some people cannot go near a church without experiencing pain because of past difficult events. Others have moved away from churches because they consider them to be institutions more concerned with structures and beliefs than being centers of spiritual vitality and personal transformation. However, it is my hope that this book does not stereotype churches as nonspiritual, just as churches in the past may have stereotyped groups outside themselves as nonspiritual. My hope is for both groups to see the possibilities of the spirit in the other. The book *Spirituality and Religion in Counseling and Psychotherapy: Diversity in Theory and Practice* (Kelly, 1995) fulfills this hope of not excluding one from the other. Kelly effectively develops a method of how a counselor, when appropriate, might work with and be present to clients' religions and spiritual energies. He describes when it is appropriate to work with religion and when it is not, in the following kinds of clients:

1. religiously committed
2. religiously loyal
3. spiritually committed

4. spiritually/religiously open
5. externally religious
6. spiritually/religiously tolerant or indifferent
7. nonspiritual/nonreligious
8. hostile to religion (pp. 136-141)

In the past, people had experiences of the divine that we might term religious or spiritual, with a resultant change of consciousness and belief. They formed communities for spiritual support, and social institutions evolved to continue their beliefs and experiences. Religion evolved with ritual, structure, and tradition as a formal way to express and carry out the group's spirituality. In due course, these groups built churches, mosques, and temples.

If being religious is to follow the beliefs and practices of an organized religious organization, then how are present organized church structures and beliefs related to spirituality? A person can belong to and even externally participate in a church and not necessarily be spiritual. For example, some people may attend a religious ritual without seeking any deeper meaning in it. In this regard, terms such as "healthy" religion versus "unhealthy" religion apply, with the assumption being that healthy religion has a spiritual growth-oriented focus and unhealthy religion focuses on the external.

Gordon Allport (1968) uses the terms *extrinsic religion* and *intrinsic religion*. If people use religion only for self-centered motives, such as the need for security or the need for status or self-esteem, then they relate extrinsically to religion. Allport sees this extrinsic motivation as immature and ultimately unhealthy. Intrinsic religion occurs if people relate to religion for a spiritual motive such as the need to reach beyond self to meet and serve God, neighbor, or religious beliefs. Intrinsic religion has a strong spiritual focus and leads to good mental health through self-transcendence.

Spirituality within religion brings to it a deeper level of consciousness. This does not mean that the external, outward expressions of religion are unimportant. Rather, they can lead us to a deeper spirit and spirituality. Faiver et al. (2001) discuss the exoteric (external) versus the esoteric (experiential) expressions of religion. One can lead and support the other.

A healthy religion facilitates and builds strong personal spirit. In *Counseling for Spiritually Empowered Wholeness,* Clinebell (1995) states that a religion is healthy or "salugenic" if it leads people to spiritual growth expanding their connections beyond and within the self. This spiritual reality leads to a nurture of the self, enhanced connections with God, with others, with nature, and a consequent enlargement of meaning, hope, and community. Hence healthy religion builds on an internal, intrinsic spirituality. Indeed, it evolves naturally from a healthy spirituality. For example, if individual spirituality is vibrant it reaches out beyond the self not only to a Higher Power but also to other connections, especially to other people in community. In other words, spirit and spirituality are expansive—not inclusive. The instinct or urge is to share our spiritual energy with others and to likewise seek the support of others in our spiritual path. Out of these experiences, groups and organizations evolve with beliefs, practices, and structures. Could such a group even become what we would term a religious organization? Religion is as natural to humans as the spirituality on which it is built. If the religion is no longer in touch with its spiritual roots, it needs to recover a healthy spirituality to stay vibrant. Religion needs spirit to overcome mere structure and externals.

Moreover, people desire to pass down their spiritual beliefs. With a healthy religion, each generation does not have to reinvent the wheel to grow spiritually. Such a religion will lead people to recognize their spiritual needs and facilitate their spiritual development through closely relating religion's ultimate meanings, symbols, and sustaining energies to people's spiritual yearnings. Expressing one's spirituality through religion can be considered a very typical human activity (Prozesky, 1984). As a human, it is as natural to be religious as it is to be spiritual.

Reflection Questions: What motivates your religious beliefs and practices? Are they healthy or unhealthy? How do they facilitate your spiritual development?

Many religions view early spiritual experiences as extraordinary or supernatural events frequently called "revelations." These revelations and/or sacred writings are seen as transcendent ways of knowing the world beyond and connecting with an ultimate being. These revelations are spiritual in that they call people to move beyond the self to find meaning, hope, and certainty in the revelation that lies beyond it. Such a religion can lead to deep feelings of ultimate well-being because it is based on a unity with divinity and mystery. Hopefully, spirituality and religion will be compatible. However, as previously discussed, this is not always the case. Whether we focus our lives on a spiritual path, in a religion, or on another philosophical path of meaning, we grow spiritually.

CORE HUMAN SPIRITUAL NEEDS

Human beings thrive through their bodies, their minds, and their spirits. If they are composed of a body, a mind with a psyche, and a spirit, they have needs in all three areas. The body needs the organic elements of food and water; the mind needs knowledge; the psyche needs the emotional elements of feelings and relationship. Finally, to become a whole person, the spirit itself has its own needs. What are these human spiritual needs? This is usually a difficult question to answer because most people rarely think of spiritual needs. They are centered on religious beliefs, practices, and rituals. However, religion is based on a *deeper spirituality* within a person. Caregivers can recognize, identify, and work with these deeper human spiritual needs.

A primary need exists for this book because many caregivers think of human needs as only physical and psychological, not spiritual. People are born with a spiritual nature, but not with automatic spiritual sight. This comes later. Most helping professionals equate spiritual needs with psychological needs. They do not see a deeper level of human spiritual needs completing psychological ones. For example, we think psychological needs arise out of low self-esteem, anger, loss, and frustration. We find it more difficult to think of spiritual needs for meaning, for hope, and for deeper connections in life and beyond. True, the spiritual need for meaning and love is not separate from the psychological need for self-esteem. However, the spiritual need for meaning and love can be seen as a deeper level or a completion of the psychological need for self-esteem. Psychological and spiritual needs are not simply equated. Spiritual needs are a deeper perspective of and/or completion of psychological needs. Spiritual needs expand and transcend psychological needs and in this process integrate and complete them (see Figure 1.2). For instance, the psychological need for self-consciousness and self-awareness finds spir-

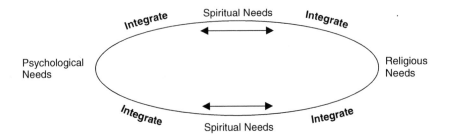

FIGURE 1.2. Integrative Function of Spiritual Needs

itual completion in meaning. The psychological need for mental health finds completion in spiritual wholeness and healing.

Unfortunately, when people do develop an awareness of spiritual needs, they usually verbalize those needs only in psychological terms. This is because they live in a psychologically focused culture and naturally reflect psychologically rather than spiritually. For example, a hospital chaplain may state that she or he, in working with a patient's anger or low self-esteem, is working with spiritual needs when these needs are more specifically and explicitly psychological needs.

The key question is: If there are specific spiritual needs, what are they, and are there specific spiritual terms to describe spiritual needs? As previously stated, spirituality is a deeper perspective or the "life principle that pervades a person's entire being, including volitional [and] emotional . . ." (Colliton, 1981, p. 492). Spiritual needs are more than psychological needs of feelings or will alone. What precisely are these spiritual needs, these deeper unifying perspectives that bring healthy integration to the person?

O'Brien (1982), in the book *Human Needs and the Nursing Process,* states that "spiritual needs are seen as involving any essential variables required for the support and variability of that element which inspires in man [or woman] the desire to transcend the realm of the material" (p. 89). Whatever leads us to rise above ourselves is spiritual. For example, people need self-confidence to move beyond the self. Self-confidence then would be a spiritual need. O'Brien's description of a spiritual need is correct, clear, and uncomplicated, but it still speaks of spiritual needs in more psychological language.

Helping professionals need a common vocabulary of spirituality to work with helpees. In the first edition of his popular book *Basic Types of Pastoral Counseling* (1966), Clinebell lists four basic spiritual needs. They are

1. to find meaning in life
2. to have a sense of the transcendent
3. to relate healthily to God, other people, and nature
4. to experience inner awareness, creativity, and freedom (p. 251)

These focus on specific aspects of spiritual need—the needs of our spiritual nature.

At a later date, a group of nurses built on Clinebell's initial work by relating spiritual needs to the area of spiritual care of hospital patients. Of particular interest is Highfield and Cason's (1983) seminal article, "Spiritual Needs of Patients: Are They Recognized?" They identified four spiritual needs that all people share:

1. The need for meaning and purpose in life
2. The need to give love
3. The need to receive love
4. The need for forgiveness, hope, and creativity (p. 188)

As part of the fourth need, people also frequently find the need for forgiveness added to the need for hope and creativity. They do not experience much hope and creativity if they feel guilty and unforgiven. So, I would summarize the fourth spiritual need as the need for forgiveness, hope, and creativity. Also, sometimes the two needs for giving and receiving love are summarized under one common spiritual need—the need for love.

These four spiritual needs inform our personalities and persons. Indeed they deepen and unify the psychological perspective of the person in that they bring completion to psychological needs. The first spiritual need for meaning gives us a sense of purpose and direction in life. It facilitates our not living in a vacuum with a sense of emptiness. If we find purpose in life, then we can usually find energy for a full life. The second and third spiritual needs to give and to receive love seem self-evident. However, our modern culture of individualism and independence creates a tremendous spiritual need for relationship and community. Finally, the fourth spiritual need for forgiveness, hope, and creativity is for many the least obvious and most difficult to recognize of our spiritual needs. Frequently today, people say how hard it is to forgive someone who has hurt them or even to forgive themselves for hurting others. Our modern psychological culture ignores this fourth spiritual need, telling us not to worry so much about forgiving others. It tells us that the important reality is to move on with our lives. It is evident that spiritual needs add a deeper perspective to the psychological needs of each individual. They bring integration and wholeness to their thinking, emotions, and behavior, indeed their whole lives.

These four core spiritual needs are indeed the foundations of the unifying spiritual principle that deeply affects who we are as people. They complete and enrich our physical, psychological, and religious needs. Take time to stop and think of these four spiritual needs in regard to yourself. Can you identify one area that is strong and one that is weak? Of these four spiritual needs, my experience is that helpers frequently need to grow more in the area of receiving love. Most are very good at giving love but find it much harder to take the time to receive love. In his book *The Art of Counseling,* Rollo May (1989) notes that many helpers have a messianic need to save the world (see "Analysis of a Typical Counselor," pp. 134-142). He thinks that spiritually, people view themselves as needing to give rather than also seeing themselves as very much needing to receive love. Do you take the time to smell the flowers and receive the love? Once you have experienced and reflected upon this fourfold model of spiritual needs in your own life, begin to use it in your one-on-one helping relationships. Use this model to reflect on and to identify with the specific spiritual needs of your helpees. Eventually, you might even use this model to identify the spiritual needs of groups and larger communities to develop programs around particular spiritual needs.

Practical Exercises

Become familiar with working with helpees' spiritual needs by doing some of the following: Watch a TV sitcom or soap opera and reflect on the various participants' spiritual needs. Listen to someone's personal story, and see whether you can determine the spiritual needs in the story. Also, notice the various stories people tell about others. These stories frequently reflect the specific spiritual needs of the individuals sharing the tales. Or you might notice the stories that you tell others. Do they reflect your own spiritual needs? Look for spiritual needs or strengths as you read human interest articles in the newspaper. In working with helpees, observe whether a psychological need, such as a need for better self-esteem, relates to a spiritual need, such as the need to give and to receive love. Spend some quiet time alone and reflect on how you might use your area of spiritual strength more effectively in helping others. How might you grow in your less-developed area of spiritual weakness (e.g., difficulty in receiving love)?

CASE STUDIES

Case Study I

Mary, an elderly woman, (1) *cares** at home for her husband with progressive Parkinson's disease. She is always available to help him with taking medications, getting dressed, and engaging in physical therapy, and is exhausted. He is (2) *getting worse,* and Mary is thinking of getting some outside help. Her husband objects, stating that it is (3) *the role of the wife* to always care for the husband. Mary does not know (4) *how long* she can continue to perform these acts for her husband. It has become too much for her.

Mary's spiritual needs and possible spiritual care follow:

1. Mary gives love and *care* to her husband. Allow her to verbalize how she does this. Is she also taking care of herself? How does she receive love and care as well as give it?
2. *Getting worse.* Mary could be experiencing fear of her husband's death and a loss of hope. Listen to her fears and, if needed, find some hope in the situation or her spirituality.
3. *Role of wife* always to care—might be expanded into a broader sense of the spiritual meaning of the role of the wife. Perhaps, if she is a Christian, Mary and her husband could reflect on how Jesus asks us to love our neighbor as ourselves. Even to care for her husband, she needs also to take care of her own needs. Encourage her to talk about her own needs as well as her husband's.

---

*Each number and word(s) in italics points to a possible spiritual need.

4. Mary does not know *how long* she can continue. This calls, perhaps for a stronger spiritual sense of hope in herself, in her God, and in the help of others. Feel her pain with her, and let Mary know that someone else understands, cares, and wants to help.

Case Study II

Julius, a forty-five-year-old man, shares that in the past year his (1) *wife and son both died*. This happened within four months of each other, the wife first with cancer and the son with congenital heart disease. Concerning his son, the father is angry with the hospital staff whom he (2) *feels did not really do their best* to revive him when his heart failed the final time. Julius states that (3) *he should have been there* to have perhaps prevented this from happening.

Julius's spiritual needs and possible spiritual care follow:

1. *Wife and son both died*—brings to Julius much grief and a strong loss of love in his life. He has a spiritual need for love and care. Allow Julius to tell his story as often as he needs to and to be in grief. He needs to share the loss of his relationships with his wife and son.
2. *Feeling that the hospital did not really do its best*—shows that Julius is perhaps looking for the spiritual meaning of what happened in the hospital. Allow him to verbalize this anger and loss. What does he want to do with it? He could also be projecting his own feelings of guilt onto the hospital.
3. *Feels that he should have been there*—shows Julius's guilt and spiritual need for self-forgiveness. Accepting Julius in this situation can facilitate his willingness to accept and forgive himself.

Case Study III

Gloria, a fifty-year-old (1) *social worker,* has been (2) *diagnosed with terminal cancer.* She worked in the hospital where she now lies sick. Her life has been one of looking out for others, including staff and patients. When the chaplain visits her, (3) *she does not speak of or share herself.* Rather, she smiles and inquires how others are doing in the hospital. People note that she is courageous and brave.

Gloria's spiritual needs and possible spiritual care follow:

1. Being a *social worker*—tells us that she has been highly involved in caring and giving love to others. Help her be open now to the spiritual need to receive love. Gloria has been strong in giving love. Can she now be more vulnerable and open to receive the love that she needs in her situation?
2. *Diagnosed with terminal cancer*—could bring denial, fear, guilt, etc. This diagnosis of a terminal illness certainly calls Gloria to examine the change and present spiritual meaning of her life. Can we be with her wherever she chooses to be in this situation? Does she have hope and any need for forgiveness and internal healing?
3. *She does not speak of or share herself*—could show her present fear and denial of her situation. Help Gloria accept this situation and at the same time attempt to move her to look at herself through an open-ended question such as, "Gloria, I am wondering what you are saying to yourself regarding your diagnosis?" Another open-ended comment might be, "I am wondering where God is in this situation with you." Gloria has a spiritual need for care and love, indeed a need at this time not so much for brave independence but a connecting interdependence. How can you help her receive the care of others and find hope and meaning in her new situation?

Analysis

Working with the four spiritual needs provides a strong resource for spiritual care. After assessing a helpee's spiritual needs, supportive work can begin with either his or her spiritual strength or spiritual lack, depending on the person. For example, if a helpee is experiencing a strong sense of fear and at the same time has a healthy spiritual and religious support system, the helper can draw upon this support to work with the fear. Also, after listening to a very distressed helpee and assessing a lack of hope, the helper could facilitate a way to develop hope to relieve the psychological pain and anguish. Since spiritual needs are deeper perspectives of psychological needs, weakness or strength in one area relates closely to weakness or strength in the other. If the helper perceives a large number of unfulfilled spiritual needs, the same will usually hold true with psychological needs. If a helpee lacks the spiritual needs of meaning, relationship, and hope, most assuredly he or she would also be facing a void in the psychological needs of self-esteem and self acceptance. Spiritual fulfillment and psychological adjustment are closely connected.

Reflection Questions: Do you think that the four areas of spiritual need clearly and precisely encompass the spiritual needs of a person? Where do you see your helpees' area or areas of greatest spiritual need? What are their spiritual strengths? What are your strengths? What area of spiritual need would you like to grow in? How do you explain the integration of psychological and spiritual needs? Do you view them as closely connected?

SPIRITUAL NEEDS IN REGARD
TO PSYCHOLOGICAL AND RELIGIOUS NEEDS

To further clarify spiritual needs, let us visualize them more specifically in regard to psychological and religious needs. Psychological needs bring individual health to the person in her or his mind and psyche; they are the "manifest data" at hand in the human person. Examples of psychological needs would be self-awareness, expression of feelings, or finding one's identity. Spiritual needs are those that transcend the material nature of the person (Kuhn, 1998). Examples would be developing a higher level of meaning and consciousness, moving beyond the self to deeper relationships and community, or experiencing love, forgiveness, and hope. They enable the human person to attain a certain state of being that reflects peace and expansiveness. As we can see in Figure 1.3, spiritual needs complete psychological needs. Higher spiritual consciousness in the person brings integration and more completion to psychological self-awareness. Love brings integration and more completion to psychological self-esteem and happiness. However, spiritual needs also facilitate and bring fulfillment to religious needs. Bringing more meaning to his or her religious beliefs brings deeper fulfillment to the person. A person's membership in a religious group brings genuine fulfillment through spiritually experiencing his or her religion as a way of life rather than simply membership in an organization. Figure 1.3 illus-

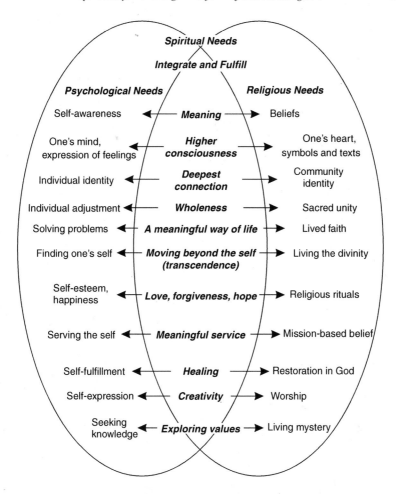

FIGURE 1.3. Integrative Function of Spiritual Needs

trates how spiritual needs integrate and complete psychological needs and fulfill religious ones.

Spiritual needs are not in addition to psychological needs, but are the depth and completion of them. They are not needs in addition to the possible religious needs of a person, but they enhance and fulfill these needs. Spirituality is an essential part of both the psychological and the religious person. However, we cannot completely contain or identify spiritual needs within one area. Rather, spiritual needs as aspects of integration are found within and between both. As such, the spiritual needs of a person are not entities apart from psychological and religious needs, but integrative principles of them both. The fulfillment of spiritual needs integrates the person psychologically and religiously. As such, assessment of spiritual needs is a natural process both for the psychologist and the religious professional.

In this regard, identifying spiritual needs or spiritual assessment lies in the area between psychology and religion, and it needs its own vocabulary. It does not merely use the classifications of psychological language, nor does it merely use theological terminology. *Spiritual language is a vocabulary between psychology and religion.* Psychological language is often clinical and categorical; likewise religious language can be abstract and otherworldly. However, the language of spiritual needs and assessment is experiential and practical. This is evident in the experiential language of spiritual needs previously discussed: the need for meaning, the need to give and receive love, and the need for hope, creativity, and forgiveness. This is only a small piece of a beginning spiritual vocabulary. Much more work needs to be done in the development of a language of spirituality, spiritual care, and spiritual assessment. George Fitchett (1993) closes his book *Assessing Spiritual Needs* by stating: "Finally, I hope that future work in spiritual assessment will help us find a meaningful language for spirituality" (p. 133). A spiritual vocabulary is needed that takes the insights of psychology and our religious traditions and speaks to the whole person in a spiritually dynamic way.

EXPANDING THE LANGUAGE OF SPIRITUAL NEEDS

What are some specific signs in people that point out the four spiritual needs we have been discussing? Obviously, helpees will not usually tell us that they have a need for meaning, for connection, or for hope and forgiveness. However, by observing a helpee's behavior and really listening to what lies beneath his or her words, we can readily identify spiritual needs and become more effective spiritual caregivers. Nurses committed to spiritual care have taken these four spiritual needs and identified certain behaviors that more readily alert the helper to the helpee's spiritual needs. Highfield and Cason (1983) developed and performed a research study to observe the relationship between the conditions and specific behaviors of patients and the four spiritual needs. They proposed that certain behaviors are signs of spiritual health and other behaviors are signs of spiritual problems. I find that some people are offended by the term *spiritual problem,* interpreting it as judgmental. It may be more preferable to use terms such as *spiritual concern* or *spiritual distress.* The following is an abbreviated version of Highfield and Cason's table (1983, p. 188), listing the signs of spiritual problems (concerns, distress) in relation to a specific spiritual need that an individual might find while working in a health care setting:

Signs of Spiritual Problems (Distress)

Need for meaning and purpose in life	Expresses that he or she has no reason to live, questions the meaning in suffering and death, and expresses despair and emotional detachment from self and peers.
Need to receive love	Expresses fear of dependence, does not call on others for help when needed, expresses guilty feelings, expresses anger with self/others, expresses resentment toward God, and expresses loss of self-value.
Need to give love	Worries about the financial status of family during hospitalization/ separation from family, and about separation from others through death.
Need for hope and creativity (forgiveness)	Exhibits overdependent behaviors, expresses anxiety about inability to pursue career, marriage, and parenting because of illness, expresses fear of therapy, and denies the reality of one's condition.

Of course, it is not practical to try to remember all these specific behaviors. This list is only an example of some typical behaviors caregivers can look for. Spiritual needs are not vague or abstract concepts, but are measurable signs observable in our helpees' behaviors, stories, and feelings. What behaviors have you observed in your helpees that show spiritual needs?

NAMING SPIRITUAL NEEDS

Objections To

Some may object to naming specific spiritual needs. They prefer to keep spirituality and spiritual care a more reserved, intuitive, and subjective process. Such, perhaps, is the path found in the formal field of spiritual direction. The spiritual director and directee focus on how God is calling and leading a person, rather than on what the particular spiritual needs of a person are. The focus of spiritual direction is on a person's journey and relationship with God, especially his or her prayer life. The spiritual director asks, "Down what path is God leading you?"

The field of spiritual care, however, focuses more on a person's specific spiritual *needs* usually in relation to a psychological concern or human problem. It is more of a clinical approach to spirituality. Nonetheless, both spiritual directors and spiritual care providers focus on a person's spiritual growth and formation. Moreover, both spiritual directors and directees can be aware of their own spiritual needs as they discern how God is leading them. Likewise, those involved in spiritual care also need to be aware of the spiritual journey and lifelong spiritual development of their helpees. The particular terminology of spiritual directors and spiritual caregivers expresses their different focuses. Spiritual caregivers would use terms such as *spiritual well-being, spiritual wellness,* and *spiritual health* in regard to the helpee. The spiritual director would use the term *spiritual direction* in regard to the directee. Finally, some spiritual caregivers may be hesitant to name spiritual needs, fearing that by naming spiritual needs in others they may categorize people, even pass judgment on their spiritual lives. They fear that caregivers will begin labeling people rather than simply accepting all helpees as beautiful children of God, no matter what their spiritual needs. Labeling is a danger that we need to be sensitive to.

Reasons For

Surely we do not want to relate to people simply as categories. I can still recall a nurse requesting me, as the chaplain, to visit the "neurotic" down the hall. Moreover, we do not want to diagnose our helpees in the way a psychologist might diagnose a client with a mental problem. But frequently, the reality is that people do not progress through life's problems until they know what is happening to them by naming it.

For example, I may feel down for a number of days without knowing why. It may be because I am afraid of failing in a school or a work project. Once I label the deeper feeling as "fear," I can specifically face the lack of courage in myself that activates the fear. When I begin to name or label a deeper feeling that is hidden, I make progress. Consequently, I can develop ways to overcome my feeling of fear. Before naming the fear, I just felt down and did not know why. Naming the problem or the feeling begins a healing process.

Faith communities acknowledge a strong healing process in the confession of sin. Naming the sin begins the process of healing. In spiritual care, I could lie in a hospital bed and feel sorry for myself, thinking it is because of my illness, and this may well be all that it is. However, if my sadness does not leave me, a competent spiritual caregiver may lead me to a deeper awareness through helping me name my fear of further losing my physical well-being or even my life. The spiritual caregiver in this situation can identify my spiritual need for hope and meaning. He or she can then work with these needs to alleviate my sadness. Ideally, the helpee by herself or himself will name what is taking place. If not, a competent helper knows how to suggest or personalize in spiritual language for the helpee what is happening.

In a real sense, once the spiritual caregiver can see and name a spiritual need in a helpee, the caregiver can facilitate a way to fulfill this spiritual need. The spiritual caregiver might facilitate hope through drawing upon the religious meaning system of the client, or simply through a strong listening presence to the helpee's sadness and worries. There is great value in naming, or at the least becoming aware of, specific spiritual needs in helpees. Spiritual needs are simply a way to think of where people are spiritually. From these needs we can identify the areas or the points to which they might grow spiritually. For example, if we discover and assess that someone lacks meaning in life, we can then more readily work with this spiritual lack and develop a possible way to help this person find deeper significance in life. If we discover that in a person's sickness he or she feels unlovable, we can help this person to see and appreciate his or her dignity as a person and a child of God. If we discover that he or she is angry and unable to give love, we can work with the anger so love can follow. If we discover a person is filled with guilt and fear, we can facilitate a way to help him or her find forgiveness and to experience freedom, hope, and creativity. In summary, working with specific spiritual needs is a much more active, supportive, and creative way to facilitate spiritual health than simply working with helpees in a general way as a friendly visitor. Paradigms of spiritual needs facilitate that we as spiritual caregivers work with the whole person in skilled and focused ways. Spiritual care, through identifying spiritual needs, makes health care, psychological care, and religious care become whole-person care. By identifying spiritual needs, we move spiritual care from intuition alone to informed spiritual care (Ivy, 1988). Identifying and expanding the language of spirituality and spiritual needs expands the whole area of spiritual care for us and for our helpees.

Reflection Questions: How do you feel about working with the spiritual needs of others? What are the reasons for and possible cautions in naming spiritual needs in others? Meet with a spiritual director and discuss the differences and similarities between spiritual direction and spiritual care.

SPIRITUAL WELL-BEING AND HEALTH

The goal of all spiritual care is spiritual well-being. Through working with spiritual needs we intentionally aim to facilitate the spiritual health of others. *Spiritual well-being* is the clinical term used to describe strong spiritual health or wellness. Spiritual well-being does not mean that our helpees' spiritual needs are ever completely met or satisfied since spiritual growth, health, and wellness are continuous processes. However, to really experience strong spiritual well-being a person would need to experience some wholeness in regard to the four spiritual needs previously outlined. *The Pocket Guide to Nursing*

Diagnoses (Kim, McFarland, and McLane, 1995) lists the defining characteristics of spiritual well-being as "relatedness, connectedness, harmony with self, others, higher power or God, and the environment" (p. 17). As such, spiritual well-being includes a healthy relationship with self, others, and the transcendent or divine beyond and deep within.

People with spiritual well-being have a feel for the meaning of their lives, a basis for love and relatedness, and a way to experience forgiveness (Peterson, 1985). Moreover, they have a sense of hope whatever their present life experience. In the end, we can feel confident that our helpees are experiencing spiritual well-being when their lack of interior peace, unresolved guilt, and feelings of loneliness, abandonment, boredom, and emptiness have been replaced with a sense of hope, connectedness, and meaning. In summary, our specific objective as spiritual caregivers is to work with the spiritual needs of our helpees toward the goal of facilitating their continued spiritual well-being. The modern world constantly reminds us to be physically and mentally healthy. We as spiritual caregivers facilitate and call others to spiritual well-being, which is the sign and gauge of their spiritual wellness and health.

Defining Characteristics Of

Carpenito (1977) defines spiritual well-being as the following:

* An inner strength that nurtures
    —Sense awareness, sacred source
    —Trust relationships, inner peace
    —Unifying force
* An intangible motivation and commitment directed toward ultimate values of love, meaning, hope, beauty, and truth
* Trust relations with or in the transcendent that provides bases for meaning and hope in life's experiences and love in personal relationships
* A meaning and purpose to existence (p. 870)

Reflection Questions: Can you give examples of spiritually healthy people who exhibit the characteristics of spiritual well-being? Where would you place yourself on a continuum of spiritual well-being?

SPIRITUAL DISTRESS AND RELIGIOUS
OR SPIRITUAL PROBLEMS

Spiritual distress describes the reality of a weakened human spirit. It is "the state in which the individual or group experiences or is at risk of experiencing a disturbance in the belief or value system that provides strength, hope, and meaning to life" (Carpenito, 1997, p. 852). In 1980, the Fourth Conference of Classification of Nursing Diagnoses defined spiritual distress as "a disruption in the life principle which pervades a person's entire being and which integrates and transcends one's biological and psychological nature" (Kim, McFarland, and McLane, 1995, p. 78). Prior to the use of this term, nurses used a three-step diagnosis of spiritual concern, spiritual distress, and spiritual despair to show the intensity of the problem. Now they use spiritual distress to encompass all three. You should decide what is better for your spiritual care work, using only the one term, spiritual distress, or using all three terms.

Spiritual distress happens to us all and need not be viewed negatively. It is really a unique opportunity for spiritual growth. The distress leads us to question our spirit and hopefully move to deeper meaning and spirituality. For example, whenever a person is sick or faces any grave crisis or serious problem in life, he or she frequently questions the deeper meaning of what is taking place. Why is this happening to me? Have I done something wrong to deserve this? Is there really a God since this is happening to me? Can my spirituality/religion grow and sustain me in this situation? Note that spiritual distress may occur even though in all other ways the person is functioning normally. For example, a graduate student of philosophy questions how one can live after death. He appears very anxious and concerned over this question. Certainly he is in spiritual distress, although he is functioning normally in other areas of his life.

Possible Interventions

When you assess that the helpee is in spiritual distress, encourage his or her expression of fearful and painful feelings through your presence and nonjudgmental active listening. Give him or her permission to discuss spiritual matters. Be open to a discussion of the meaning of his or her life in this situation. Encourage storytelling by encouraging the helpee to share his or her stories drawing upon times he or she found meaning in the past. This will help put the present situation in a greater perspective. Problem solve toward new spiritual understanding with the helpee. Offer to pray with or read to him or her. Stay silently with the helpee's pain as needed. For further discussion, see Kim, McFarland, and McLane (1995) and Carpenito (1997).

I find it interesting and significant that the American Psychiatric Association added the term *religious or spiritual problem* to its diagnostic manual in 1994. In the past, many psychologists simply ignored the whole area of religion and spirituality in their treatment. Even worse, some viewed religion as pathology. They now use the term *religious or spiritual problem* to describe "examples include[ing] distressing experiences that involve loss or questioning of faith, problems associated with conversion to a new faith, or questioning of spiritual values that may not be related to an organized church or religious institution" (American Psychological Association, 1994, p. 685). These terms now enable psychological professionals to refer explicitly to religion and spirituality in their treatment plans.

To conclude, spiritual caregivers can also think of and plan spiritual interventions in terms of spiritual distress or religious or spiritual problems. Moreover, by adding to this process an explicit language of spirituality, we can become more aware of our helpees' spiritual needs and better facilitate their spiritual well-being.

CONCLUSION

To identify spiritual needs in caregiving, whether the caregiving is physical, psychological, or religious, leads to whole-person care. In our weight-conscious society, when we think of health and beauty, we look at our bodies and their physical appearance and health. When we are overweight, we react emotionally or psychologically to our overeating with feelings of disappointment, guilt, and shame. To help solve our weight problems, we first look to the latest scientific and technological advances and recommendations on how to improve diet. We may also talk with a psychological counselor about our fears and concerns. Last, if at all, do we focus on the spiritual part of our overeating, the meaning beneath it. However, to face our deeper issues with weight, we may decide to join a spiritually focused support group. This group's focus on a Higher Power or God can lead us to identify our spiritual lack and needs and to trust a power outside ourselves. Moreover, as we participate in this support community, we learn to accept care and love from others in the group, to love ourselves as we are, and eventually to forgive ourselves and to find hope. This process of internal spiritual healing may lead us to lose weight and/or love ourselves as we are. It leads us to spiritual well-being with or without a weight loss.

Many people still lead soulless lives of "quiet desperation," looking for deeper spiritual connection within and beyond themselves. In this process, we say that we need a joining together of the whole person: body, mind, and spirit. The body and mind are never really healed and made whole without healing the third, the spirit. Until now we have followed the model of body first, mind second, and sometimes spirit third. Have you ever asked yourself why spirit is always listed third if it is listed at all? Will we ever see the order with spirit, body, and mind? For spirit is the life principle that completes, integrates, and fuses the body and the mind. Should it not be placed first? St. Paul, at the end of the first letter to the Thessalonians, speaks of spirit first: "may you all be kept safe and blameless, spirit, soul [mind], and body . . ." (1 Thessalonians, 5:23).*

As we have seen in this chapter, spirituality is the integrating core element of human experience. It is essential to make spirituality more obvious and accessible for people, through developing and using a specific language of spiritual needs and care. It need not be viewed as a vague or mysterious concept. Through identifying spiritual needs and naming them, it will be possible to respond more openly to those needs. Moreover, spiritual care will be more widely accepted and respected if we have a body of terms that all helpers, whether psychological or religious, can recognize and use. Consequently, both psychological and religious care will become more genuinely integrated with spiritual care. Our human nature leads us to continually seek spiritual well-being whether we live and speak of our spirituality in human or religious language. Our work as holistic caregivers is to make spirituality less hidden and to bring it out into the light of day to facilitate spiritual growth. The spirit renews us with vitality and joy. We celebrate this spiritual birthright together as humans and children of God.

---

*Biblical references from Jones, A. (Ed.). (1996). *The Jerusalem Bible*. New York: Doubleday & Co., Inc.

Chapter 2

Spiritual Assessment

FOUNDATIONS

Spiritual assessment is an appraisal process for determining the spiritual needs of an individual or an organization. Helpers and helpees do not easily envision life in spiritual terms, thus spiritual assessment presents a unique challenge. It does not automatically happen in the helping professions. The helper needs to actively intend it or work at it. This is true for both counselors and religious professionals. For example, it is easier to assess others' lack of psychological self-esteem than their spiritual lack of hope and meaning. They do not have the vocabulary to think of helpees in spiritual terms. However, more and more helping professionals are eager to learn how to think in spiritual concepts and to use spiritual vocabulary in their work. In fact, one of the most important long-term goals of the present-day interest, study, and research into spiritual assessment is the development of a common language of spirituality that helping professionals can draw upon in their work. The counselor or psychologist needs a vocabulary to make a holistic assessment of a person that includes both the spiritual dimension as well as the psychosocial. Likewise, the religious caregiver reaches for terminology to assess the spiritual dimension that flows from and supports religious beliefs and practices.

Helping professionals are looking toward the process of spiritual assessment as a more explicit and intentional method to surface spirituality in their work with helpees. As previously stated, strong spiritual care, spiritual healing, and spiritual development do not naturally or automatically happen. Physical growth, however, does happen naturally. Psychological growth takes place as well. As we develop psychologically in our interpersonal interactions with family and friends, spirituality usually lies more dormant until it is intentionally and explicitly acted upon. It needs to be more consciously developed.

A core area of spirituality is meaning. Developing a strong sense of meaning in one's life requires an intentional effort. The helper may inquire about the possible meaning found in a helpee's situation. This question on the part of the helper may lead to a more intentional effort on the helpee's part to examine his or her sense of meaning or spirituality. Spiritual care indeed requires an intentional effort both on the part of the helper and the helpee.

The Human Process of Growth

The following list shows the progression and interactive process of human development leading up to and joined with more intentional spiritual development.

- Increasing physical growth
- Emergent interpersonal psychological growth
- Intentional, conscious spiritual growth

SPIRITUAL ASSESSMENT AND THE PSYCHOLOGICAL HELPING PROFESSIONAL

At this time in the history of caring for people psychologically, why do we hear a stronger call for the development of a process of spiritual assessment? Perhaps it is because counselors are rightly realizing that helping and counseling is a spiritual process as well as a psychological one. They have always known that their helpees have psychological needs to explore feelings, to recover a healthy self-image, to work with their losses and fears, to have a sense of personal autonomy. To assess these they have developed the clinical language used in the psychological classification system of the *Diagnostic and Statistical Manual of Mental Disorders,* Fourth Edition (APA, 1994). Classifications such as "generalized anxiety disorder" or "a major depressive disorder" are necessary and useful both for the client and the counselor. They explain to the helpees reasons for feeling the way they do. Moreover, they enable the psychologist to develop a better treatment plan to follow. Now, however, counselors are also seeing the whole person beyond the psychological. They are taking a broader contextual view of the helpee. The client with a DSM-IV classification lives in a wider context of some type of spirit, spirituality, or meaning needed to survive, much less thrive. The client needs hope and a sense of belonging to the universe, moments of moving beyond self. Spiritual assessment appraises these existential needs that facilitate a process of holistic counseling. A spiritual assessment of the client enables the counselor to empathize more fully with the total life experience of the client. It means examining the client's life more as story with meaning rather than focusing only on the problem. It means empathizing with the client's connections to life, healing, and growth.

SPIRITUAL ASSESSMENT AND THE RELIGIOUS HELPING PROFESSIONAL

Most religious professionals have moved away from any explicit spiritual assessment of the person. The pastor or priest confessor might morally assess or admonish the person in regard to sin but usually does not think in terms of intentionally assessing the spiritual needs of the parishioner. Perhaps this is a reaction to recent centuries of Christianity in which people were categorized and even judged according to the sins that they had committed. For several centuries, the priest confessor used penitential books that listed classifications of sins and proper penance for them. The priest who categorized sins in a religiously oriented culture was similar to the clinical psychologist in today's psychological culture who now uses a book to classify mental disorders. Religious workers today, perhaps because of the fear of returning to a classification system of faults and sins, have avoided any kind of spiritual assessment process. In fact, I share this fear when I see the term *spiritual diagnosis* used rather than *assessment.* I prefer to use the term *spiritual assessment* to avoid the stronger sense of classifying people that diagnosis connotes. Many authors, such as Fitchett in his book *Assessing Spiritual Needs* (1993), use both terms interchangeably.

In reality, the religious helper has used a more intangible and intuitive approach to spirituality and spiritual assessment. The religious helper innately develops a feel for what is happening spiritually with the helpee. There is usually no standard or model of spiritual needs to relate this feeling to. The traditional spiritual director is a case in point. Malony (1996) states that he has never seen any portion of a book in spiritual direction devoted to spiritual assessment. Rather than assess individual spiritual needs, the spiritual director attempts to discern where God is in the directee's life or how God is speaking to the directee. It is a way to surface how God is calling the helpee rather than the spiritual director assessing the spiritual needs of the helpee or the helpee determining his or her spiritual needs. The spiritual life is seen more as a journey with God rather than a person's state of spiritual awareness and well-being. It is more of a heart-to-heart relationship with one's God. The spiritual director wants directees to get out of their heads and into their hearts to experience their God.

However, is spirituality also linked to our heads, our minds that bring up a clearer awareness of our spiritual needs? As such, spirituality is also a clinical science. Indeed, spiritual care and spiritual assessment have become more clinical terms—more useful, it seems, in settings such as pastoral care and counseling, in a hospital, nursing home, or hospice. In fact, as we have already seen, it was nurses first and later health care chaplains who began the process of the spiritual assessment of their patients. Chaplains are today the primary religious professionals who use spiritual assessment. However, my hope is that spiritual assessment will become a more inclusive, normal part of all pastoral and spiritual care. Spirituality and spiritual care can be both of the head and of the heart. Both the intuitive heart-to-heart relationship and the more scientific clinical path of spiritual needs' assessment are valuable (Figure 2.1).

The pastor or religious worker observes many stumbling blocks that keep people from a closer relationship with God (Bergin, 1988). These blocks might be physical, such as suffering; psychological,

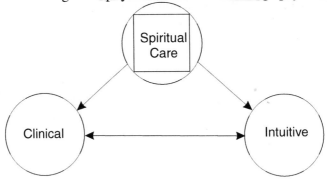

FIGURE 2.1. Inclusive Spiritual Assessment

such as emotional suffering, anger, stress, addiction, and loneliness; or spiritual, such as inability to pray, a negative image of God, and weak belief. Determining and working with the spiritual needs within physical, psychological, and spiritual blocks could alleviate them. For example, a helpee in distress might say, "My faith got me through it." This statement shows the effectiveness of a person's spirituality in dealing with distress. Assessing a need for meaning in the life of the helpee and then developing a spiritual or religious sense of meaning can enable such a helpee to work through suffering. In this case, the fulfillment of a spiritual need for deeper meaning in suffering was a path to spiritual perseverance and growth. In essence, the practice in pastoral care of identifying the stumbling blocks to spiritual growth and wellness clearly relates to a process of assessment of spiritual needs. Religious workers can use models of spiritual assessment that clearly show how a person's spiritual needs are not blocks but indeed stepping-stones to spiritual wellness.

Reflection Questions: Discuss how you view spirituality and spiritual care. Can you begin a regular practice of intentionally focusing on your own and others' spiritual needs? Or do you think that spirituality just happens intuitively? As a psychological professional, how might you view your work as involving holistic spiritual care as well as psychological helping? Do you see any value in doing a spiritual assessment? As a religious professional, can you explain how spirituality and spiritual needs enter into your practice? Do you see any value in doing a spiritual assessment? Are you fearful of categorizing people when doing a spiritual assessment? How might you avoid this?

THE BASIC PROCESS OF SPIRITUAL ASSESSMENT

Spiritual assessment is not so much determining a diagnosis as it is developing a parameter or perspective on how we view the person based on particular spiritual needs. If we imagine spiritual assessment as a range between two points on a line, we might say that spiritually the person seems to be at such and such a point and the person might move to a point farther along the line. For example, in regard to one's spiritual need to receive love, we might make a spiritual assessment that a person is very limited in giving love to self. This particular person feels lovable only when working with and doing good deeds for others. We might assess for this person the possibility of loving self just as one is without basing one's self-love primarily on one's accomplishments. In this case the person might move on the continuum from self-love dependent upon accomplishments to self-love based on self-acceptance as he or she is (Figure 2.2).

Nash (1990), in the article "Life's Major Issues," speaks of doing spiritual assessment through contrasting "major polarities of spiritual issues that all persons struggle with throughout their lives" (p. 4). He lists nineteen such issues:

1. Dread → Courage
2. Aloneness → Unity
3. Helplessness → Power
4. Bondage → Freedom
5. Greed → Charity
6. Brokenness → Wholeness
7. Curse → Blessing
8. Foolishness → Wisdom
9. Guilt → Grace
10. Injustice → Justice
11. Despair → Hope
12. Apathy → Compassion
13. Revenge → Mercy
14. War → Peace
15. Faithlessness → Faithfulness
16. Misery → Joy
17. Arrogance → Humility
18. Ingratitude → Gratitude
19. Meaninglessness → Fullness of life (From "Life's Major Issues" by Roy B. Nash, 1990. *The Caregiver Journal,* Vol. 7, p. 8. Reprinted by permission of the Association of Professional Chaplains.)

We see then that the process of spiritual assessment is not categorizing people but rather viewing people on a range or a continuum of spiritual needs and growth. Is it possible for you to think of your

$$\longrightarrow$$

Dependent Self-Acceptance ⟶ Self-Acceptance As He or She Is

FIGURE 2.2. Continuum of Acceptance

helpees in this way? If so, you are doing spiritual assessment. The habit of spiritual assessment is to stand back, indeed to take at least a brief time to reflect on your helpees' spiritual needs in regard to where they are and where they might go.

Practical Exercises

Follow as a model of spiritual assessment either Nash's paradigm of spiritual issues or the four core spiritual needs discussed in Chapter 1. Reflect upon one of these models with regard to your helpees. Or perhaps develop a brief model of spiritual needs for the people with whom you work. To grow in using a process of spiritual assessment, work toward identifying spiritual needs in people as they watch TV, view a video, or read the paper or a book. If you use Nash's model, contrast both ends of the continuum in relation to spiritual needs. As Nash (1990) reflects, do not avoid staying with people in painful or negative feelings. If we can face and enter into the shadows and not run away from them, light will follow. Where do people stand as far as their spiritual needs, and where might they go?

The Four Possible Focuses of Caregiving

Spiritual assessment and care are carried out within the wider holistic care of a person's body, mind, emotions, and spirit. Before entering into spiritual assessment and care, the caregiver needs to determine whether the helpee needs or even desires spiritual care. The caregiver initially needs to assess the kind of care a particular helpee needs at the time. I (Topper, 1996) see spiritual care as one of four possible focuses of caring for the whole person. Briefly these four focuses are (1) *social-friendly care,* (2) *helping-psychological care,* (3) *spiritual care,* and (4) *ritual care.* Let us examine in more detail each of these four focuses of caring for the whole person.

Social-Friendly Care

A friendly relationship (What is happening?) focus on

- external subjects
- sharing experiences
- people in general
- being pleasant, positive

Helping-Psychological Care

A psychological relationship (How are you doing?) focus on

- one's thinking and feeling
- the person sharing self
- the person sharing painful concerns

Spiritual Care

A spirited relationship (What is the deeper meaning of all this?) focus on

- sense of meaning and purpose
- connections, the need to give and receive love
- sense of strength and hope
- spiritual/faith support system

Ritual Care

A relationship of presence (Can we commemorate, pray? How can we celebrate?) focus on

- meditation and prayer
- signs and symbols
- readings and scriptures
- visualization

The helper, depending upon his or her role and observation of the helpee and the situation, chooses or intends one of the four focuses of care. The counselor and psychologist usually look primarily to psychological care with its problem resolution and personality change and growth. Along with psychological care, they may secondarily also intentionally integrate spiritual care into this psychological focus for support and at times even problem resolution. Religious caregivers also frequently focus on problem resolution, but they more intentionally focus on spiritual care using the spiritual resources of their religious traditions. At the social-friendly level of caring, a friendly visitor's focus is simply caring conversation with helpees. This kind of care is a friendly visit exchanging information and experiences. The helper who has the need always to be positive and upbeat probably stays almost totally in this area of care. At the psychological/helping level we focus on *how* our helpees are personally doing rather than simply sharing information and ideas. We look more toward their sharing of themselves and their concerns, how they think and feel. At the spiritual level we focus on the *deeper meaning* of what is happening with our helpees. We discuss their sense of meaning in regard to the issues they are discussing, their sense of connection to self and others around them, and their deepest sense of connection and how it relates to their concerns. At the ritual level we use signs and symbols pointing toward a larger surrounding reality and sometimes even a wondrous presence involved in what is happening with them.

Simply and briefly stated, in a typical hospital visit, a pastor may visit with his or her parishioner first caring about what is happening with the patient and his or her family, and also perhaps sharing church news. Hopefully, this social-friendly type of visit would establish a connection with the patient and offer support and encouragement. Second, as the pastor enables the patient to really talk about self and how he or she feels in the present sickness and situation, the pastor would be facilitating helping-psychological care. This is true because the person is talking and sharing himself or herself. It is not just a mutual friendly conversation. The pastor does more listening and the helpee more talking. Third, as the pastor helps the person to personalize the meaning of what is happening to him or her in the light of faith or the deeper connections in life, the pastor would be participating in spiritual care. The person is looking at his or her situation from a much deeper perspective. Fourth, when the pastor prays or performs a church ceremony with the patient, he or she would be facilitating ritual care.

Reflection Questions: Do you understand the difference between each of the four areas of caregiving? In your role as a helper, what is the typical focus of caregiving that is expected of you? Do you stay in only one area of caregiving? Does this "four focuses of caring" model encourage and show you a way to expand your focuses of caregiving to other areas?

This fourfold model can help you to be more reflective and intentional concerning the type of caregiving that you give to others. Be more conscious of what is actually taking place with the helpee and choose the kind of care needed. Using this model can prevent you from only focusing on one area of care such as always being a friendly visitor. People expect more than just a friend or comforter in a religious worker today (Oates, 1982). They expect spiritual help. Hopefully this model may enable all of us to move more intentionally toward spiritual care when needed. Psychologists or counselors can help clients personalize their concerns and issues with an enhanced spiritual perspective. Through this model, a religious professional who frequently uses ritual care can integrate more spiritual care into the ritual through leading helpees to the spiritual meaning and healing within these rituals. Moreover, she or he can also facilitate helping-psychological care through empathizing with helpees' pain as she or he prays with them.

The following example of working with a person with a terminal illness demonstrates this model more clearly. First, we would want to know at least a little about the person, of what is happening in his or her life. In this process we might even share a bit of ourselves in order to help the person relate to us. However, our primary focus here as helpers would not be on social-friendly care through sharing information and experiences, but rather focusing on the needs of the person we are helping. Second, we might move into the psychological focus on how the person is thinking and feeling in regard to his or her terminal illness. We might wonder what the fears of the person are and how we as helpers might help him or her deal with them. Third, what would enable us to be effective spiritual caregivers is whether or not we can help the individual personalize the illness in regard to his or her spiritual needs. We might think of the person's fear and wonder or ask who or what is his or her primary source of strength and hope at this time. What is the real meaning of what is happening? If the person has a spiritual or religious tradition, does this tradition or God say anything to him or her? Fourth, at some time during the process, we might facilitate a ritual of healing certainly at least for internal spiritual healing of fear and an experience of forgiveness and hope. If the person has a religious tradition, he or she could draw on the traditional rituals of his or her faith community. From this model, we can see then how we can choose and facilitate a focus of care that each person needs at a particular time. As you use the model, you will become more aware how all four focuses connect and intermingle with one another. Individuals do not necessarily move chronologically from one area to the next. Each area integrates the others and they all interconnect. However, at any given time, the helper will probably spend most of the time in one of the focuses.

A BEGINNING MODEL OF SPIRITUAL ASSESSMENT

Assessing Spiritual Needs Through a Listening Conversation

Spiritual assessment and care is a developing process. As we focus on the helpee's spirituality, where does the helper begin? Ultimately how does the helper proceed? What is the goal of the assessment and care?

An initial effective process of spiritual assessment can take place simply through conversation with our helpees. This is an indirect informal process rather than a formal assessment with a questionnaire or a clinical instrument. It happens through good listening to the helpee. Reflecting upon their stories and feelings, we look for the spiritual needs within their narratives using a model of spiritual needs that we are familiar with ahead of time. I have committed to memory for this kind of exploration the model of four core spiritual needs previously discussed. Normally, using this model during a helping conversation enables the helper to begin to ascertain the spiritual needs of the helpee. This model usually enables me to describe what is happening spiritually with the helpee and also to begin to facilitate strategies and goals to respond to the spiritual needs.

Hence, spiritual assessment begins as an intuitive process of listening and having hunches about the helpee. As the conversation continues it gradually becomes more informed and clinical (Ivy, 1987.). As we listen we begin to interpret spiritual needs in regard to the model we have chosen. We move from intuition to information, to deeper empathy and insight. We move from a limited spiritual assessment to a more comprehensive one.

For example, a person shares several stories of himself or herself, trying to reach out to others. Depending upon the situation, we may assess this as a spiritual need to receive love. Another helpee speaks of fear of failure and we may assess this as a spiritual need for hope. Of course this process of assessment needs to be a collaborative process. We do not simply judge helpees by interpreting for them their spiritual needs. Hopefully through their conversations they will come to see their own spiritual needs, although they usually will not think of them in that way. The question for ourselves is whether we can help them see the deeper meaning of what is happening with them. Meaning is where the spiritual focus is found in any problem.

Use of Open-Ended Questions

If the helpee, or for that matter the helper, has a difficult time touching or integrating spirituality into the helping situation, an *open-ended question* may be useful. In fact, I think that it is very advantageous for a helper to have in his or her mind one or two open-ended questions about spirituality. For example, I might ask, "Where do you find the most help and support in this situation?" Or, "I am wondering where your Higher Power or God might be for you in this situation." If the person says that he or she has no meaning in life, I might ask him or her to look back to a time when he or she had meaning in life. It is frequently difficult for the helpee to explicitly surface his or her spirituality or spiritual experience of life. An open-ended question from the helper can facilitate this process.

The following are some open-ended questions based on our model of four core spiritual needs that you may find useful. Several of these questions come from or are paraphrases of lists of questions found in Dossey (1998) and Stoll (1979).

Need for Meaning

- What is the most important or powerful thing in your life?
- What gives your life meaning?

- What brings joy and peace into your life?
- What does your spirituality or religion say to you in your present situation?
- What do you do to feel alive and full of spirit?

Need to Give Love

- How do you reach out to others?
- Can you tell others what you think and feel?
- What are some of the loving things that you do for others?
- Which is easier for you, to give or to receive love?

Need to Receive Love

- How do you feel when others care for you?
- Who are the significant people in your life and can you ask for help when you need it?
- How do you receive peace and love from your spirituality or faith?

Need for Hope, Creativity, and Forgiveness

- How does a spirit of hope enter into your life?
- How are you in touch with your creativity?
- What does forgiveness mean to you?
- How do you feel forgiven by others, or by your Higher Power and/or God?
- When have you been able to forgive others?

Do any of these questions appeal to you? As a caveat, please note that because of this list of questions, the helper may think that the main process of spiritual assessment is simply asking a list of questions, and inquiring about spiritual needs. However, the process of spiritual assessment is listening to the person's story over time, not continually asking questions of him or her. The questions are ideas for helpers to reflect upon and material to work with. We want to do a spiritual assessment, not have a spiritual investigation, which appears to take place when too many questions are asked. Moreover, when the helper asks too many questions, the helper may come across either as a private detective type or the spiritual expert who, once he or she has the information, can solve the problem for the helpee. Rather, we want to facilitate the helpee to recognize her or his spiritual need and to discover her or his own wisdom and internal strength in relating to these needs.

By using this model, I find that I can usually begin to ascertain whether the helpee is experiencing spiritual health or well-being; or whether he or she is experiencing a spiritual concern, spiritual distress, or spiritual despair. Especially if the helpee strongly lacks the first spiritual need of meaning and purpose in life, he or she frequently experiences spiritual distress lacking spiritual fulfillment in the three other areas of spiritual needs. If the person can find meaning in life, he or she can usually adjust to life. As someone once said, "If I have a reason why, I can put up with any how." I have also found that the more a person lacks in more than one of these four spiritual needs, the more psychological concerns the helpee tends to have. Obviously, if he or she lacks both self-love and love from others and also has no sense of hope in life, the helpee will have significant psychological issues with self-esteem, healthy assertiveness, being in touch with his or her feelings, etc. In a reverse of this process, Malony (1996) states "that an increase in spirituality [fulfillment of spiritual needs] is positively related to an increase in emotional well being . . ." (p. 249) or psychological fulfillment.

Reflection Questions: Do you view spiritual assessment as a formal process with questions and survey instruments? Can you also envision doing spiritual assessment through an informal conversational process? If you have not already done so, develop open-ended questions that you might employ with helpees to access the area of spirituality in their lives. Reflect on the possible relationship of spiritual needs and emotional health. How might they go together?

Case Studies

The following are conversations with two helpees. Each case study includes the helper's later reflection upon the helpees' conversations based on the four spiritual needs. The first case study is a man of strong Christian faith in his late seventies who is a widower with three adult, married children. A few days previous to the chaplain's visit, he unexpectedly found out that he has an aggressive cancer. His possibilities for survival are slim, but the doctor holds out the hope that if the cancer has not grown too large, an operation may remove it; otherwise he has only a short time to live. The elderly man has elected to have the surgery the following day. After meeting with him and reflecting on the model of four spiritual needs, the helper assesses the following:

- *The need for meaning.* The elderly gentleman speaks of facing the operation knowing that Jesus will be with him. Many people are praying for him. He has talked with the surgeon and knows what is happening. He has chosen the operation as a last chance.
- *The need to give love.* He shares the pain and story of his cancer openly with others and is grateful for people stopping by to see him. He courageously talks with others.
- *The need to receive love.* When the helper looks around the room, the helper sees flowers and cards everywhere. The phone frequently rings. The elderly man receives much love.
- *The need for hope, creativity, and forgiveness.* He is positively entering into the operation. He spoke earlier of hope in Jesus and he restates this hope whatever the outcome. For now he trusts in the surgeon.

This case shows that, unless he is in complete denial of what is happening to him, the man has strong fulfilled spiritual needs in all four areas. He has meaning through facing exactly what is happening and through his faith in Jesus. He continues to give love by not closing up with fear but openly sharing his story of cancer with others. He receives much love from his friends and many cards and visitors. He has a strong sense of hope in Jesus whatever the outcome and a sense of trust that the surgeon is competent and will make the right decisions during surgery. He indeed has a strong sense of spiritual well-being, despite the diagnosis of cancer. The helper's spiritual care response would be to continue to support and sustain him in fulfilling his spiritual needs during this desperate situation. We will expand on his story later.

The second case study is a single woman in her sixties with serious heart complications. She is in the coronary care unit of a hospital. She is also an alcoholic who has been sober for ten years. She wants to talk about her present fears and her life. Through conversations with her, the spiritual caregiver assesses the following:

- *The need for meaning.* The woman speaks frequently of her involvement with Alcoholics Anonymous (AA). Through its twelve-step program she has found meaning and made her life worthwhile. She never found this meaning in the church of her youth. There she learned that God was a harsh, cruel God. AA has taught her to trust in the Higher Power who gets you through each day one at a time. This she is doing now with her serious heart disease.
- *The need to give love.* She gives love to her friends at AA. Once again, she was never able to achieve this in her church. AA is a closely knit group. She feels at home.
- *The need to receive love.* She receives love and acceptance from her many friends and family. They give her much support.
- *The need for hope, creativity, and forgiveness.* Although she has done the AA step of making an assessment of her past wrong deeds and sought to make amends, she still worries whether God can really forgive her. She states that she has done too much in the past for God's forgiveness. Because she does not feel completely forgiven, she lacks a basic sense of hope as she faces her serious illness.

In this case we can see a woman who has found a strong sense of meaning in following the steps of AA. She has also found a gentler image of God. She has made many friends and through regularly attending the meetings she gives and receives much love. However, of the four spiritual needs, she lacks a strong sense of hope because she feels unforgiven for her past. She has a spiritual need to really experience forgiveness and consequently find deeper hope in this life and more peacefully face the next life. What might be our spiritual care response to help hope surface in her heart?

The 7 × 7 Holistic, Functional Model of Spiritual Assessment

The model of four core spiritual needs is excellent for spiritual assessment by itself. However, psychological professionals need a broader model of assessment than one that includes only spiritual assessment.

For them spiritual assessment is viewed within the whole psycho-social assessment of the person. George Fitchett's (1993) expanded 7 × 7 model of spiritual assessment is such a model. It includes seven holistic dimensions of the person including the psychological and other human dimensions as well as seven spiritual dimensions. It closely relates the holistic and the spiritual dimensions of the person. The following is a list of the particular dimensions.

Fitchett's

Holistic Dimensions	**Spiritual Dimensions**
Medical	Beliefs and Meaning
Psychological	Vocation and Consequences
Psychosocial	Experience and Emotion
Family Systems	Courage and Growth
Ethnic and Cultural	Ritual and Practice
Societal Issues	Community
Spiritual	Authority and Guidance*

(From *Assessing Spiritual Needs* by George Fitchett, 1993, p. 42. Reprinted by permission of the Association of Professional Chaplains.)

As previously discussed, one of the dangers of any assessment process is that after a time, we may tend to perceive the helpee as a category rather than a person. This 7 × 7 model as a multidimensional model helps us to avoid categorizing the individual under one dimension. It enables counseling professionals to see spiritual assessment within the more traditional assessment process that they are accustomed to. They primarily view their helpees from a psychological focus, viewing the person in regard to self and others. What is the person's sense of self, how does the helpee interact with others, how does her or his ethnic and cultural background affect her or his personality? And together with these, how does the spiritual dimension of the helpee's life presently impact him or her? Notice also how Fitchett's spiritual dimensions functionally expand and specify more precisely the spiritual needs of the four core spiritual needs model. Meaning is functionally expanded into how a person lives belief and meaning through his or her vocation and its consequences. The need

---

*Fitchett has a good example of the use of his model in his article "Linda Kraus and the Lap of God," *Second Opinion, 20*(4), p. 41, 1995.

to give and to receive love is functionally expanded into experience and emotion and the need for community. The need for hope is functionally expanded into the need for courage and continued growth.

One of the chief criteria for a good spiritual assessment is that it be functional as opposed to only substantive. Substantive spirituality is what a person believes; functional spirituality is how a person lives his or her meaning or beliefs. In spiritual assessment, both psychological and religious professionals look toward how people function in their spirituality, not just the substance of meaning. A functional spiritual assessment looks to a more optimal way of life and increased spirit for the person. Fitchett's expanded 7 × 7 model gives us a total functional framework.

Reflection Questions: Similar to our case studies, can you listen to a person's conversation or story and identify the spiritual needs behind the story? Think of your own past and present experiences and life stories. Can you recognize the key spiritual needs in them? Do you see any life pattern in your own spiritual needs? Similar to Fitchett's functional model, can you assess a person's spiritual needs in regard to his or her other holistic needs such as self-esteem and family relationships?

Chapter 3

The Process of Spiritual Care

Spiritual care stands as the whole process or umbrella over and the extension and application of spiritual assessment. Through spiritual assessment the caregiver identifies the spiritual needs of the helpee. However, spiritual assessment is only one important piece or part of the whole process of spiritual care. Looking at the whole perspective of spiritual care, we can determine four distinct steps. These steps do not always proceed in order, nor are they always employed.

A typical spiritual care process might progress in the following way. A psychological or a religious professional meets with a helpee, actively listens to his or her concerns, and develops a helping relationship. Out of this relationship, a clearer picture of an issue, a concern, or a problem arises. As we continue to focus on the helpee and the concern, we first address the kind of care needed, whether a social-friendly relationship, a helping-psychological relationship, spiritual care, or ritual care. Second, if spiritual care is the needed focus of helping and also wanted on the part of the helpee, assess spiritual need. Once this is identified, we would attempt to facilitate the helpee reframing his or her concern within a spiritual perspective as a beginning step toward spiritual healing and growth to the helpee. Third, based on the identified particular spiritual need(s), we would reflect on and develop the purpose or goal of spiritual care for this person and a strategy to reach that goal. The spiritual goal might be a need for internal healing, a need for support and being sustained, a need for guidance, or a need for reconciliation. Fourth, if desired by the helpee, we would use his or her belief systems and its practices for even more complete integrated spiritual support and care. Each of these four steps is examined next.

STEP ONE: ADDRESS THE FOCUS
OF CARE NEEDED

As he or she listens to a person's story, the spiritual caregiver needs to determine whether spiritual care is the focus of helping that the helpee presently needs or wants. This determination is based on our earlier model in Chapter 2 of the focus of care needed at a particular time. There may be other more pressing needs such as psychological needs with concerns for self-acceptance, feelings of anger, and low self-esteem. Moreover, although there may be strong spiritual needs, the helpee may not want to go to that place. He or she may want or need only a friendly conversation with perhaps a prayer or a simple blessing ritual rather than a discussion related to spiritual needs or a conversation about his or her relationship with a Higher Power or God. To determine the focus of care the helper can use the fourfold model previously discussed.

With regard to the two case studies in Chapter 2, the elderly man with aggressive cancer and the woman with a heart condition, of the four focuses of caring, which do they presently need? The elderly man has found out that his cancer is inoperable. Despite this news, he continues to live in peace because of his strong spirituality. In his case, this carries over into psychological strength exhibited with his courage in facing and accepting his own death. He has many friends. He prays and meaningfully participates in the rituals of his faith. As previously stated, he does not have any one focus of especially strong need of care. To a large extent, even in his present terminal situation, he experiences psychological health and spiritual well-being. The spiritual caregiver's response is to give him support in each area of care (social, psychological, spiritual, and ritual) as he needs it, to continue to listen to his story, pains, and joys as they unfold. If he continues to have the energy and the time, the elderly man might want to do some life review and reflect on the role of his family, friends, and God in his life. He might reflect more closely on what have been the most meaningful experiences of his life. Particularly religious or ritual care might continue to spiritually sustain him and bring him stronger internal healing. With the members of his family, friends, and faith community gathered around him, the man could pray with the scriptures and rituals of the church. As his disease progresses, sometimes church hymns or prayers listened to on cassette sustain people in sickness and dying.

With regard to the woman with the heart condition, her serious condition remains precarious. What focus or focuses of care does she most need—psychological, spiritual, or ritual? It appears that she needs both psychological help to accept her situation and spiritual care to heal her need for personal forgiveness of her past and to find hope in the present and the future. The helper, in completely accepting the woman with her guilt feelings, offers her an accepting forgiveness. This forgiveness can hopefully bring internal healing and peace. Also psychologically we might wonder because she cannot easily accept forgiveness of God for her past, does she have a need to feel unforgiven? Where might this come from? Psychologically, can we help her talk and examine her fear of forgiveness more fully? Spiritually, we might point out the meaning of forgiveness in the twelve steps of AA. We might share scriptures of God's ever-present forgiveness and love. How can we help her experience His forgiveness? Ritually, we might pray God's words of forgiveness with and for her.

STEP TWO: ASSESS SPIRITUAL NEEDS

Chapter 2 explains this important step in detail, identifying the four core spiritual needs. Returning again to its two case studies, we saw how we can make a spiritual assessment through listening to another's story in regard to her or his spiritual needs. Through a good spiritual assessment, we move from intuition to insight and information about the helpee's spiritual needs. As a result, we can reach out with a spiritual care response to the specific spiritual needs of the helpee whether they be need for meaning, need to give love, need to receive love, or need for forgiveness, hope, and creativity.

STEP THREE: DETERMINE THE GOALS OF SPIRITUAL CARE

Our spiritual care responses to particular spiritual needs can be summarized and specified in four long-range goals of spiritual care.

They are healing, sustaining, guiding, and reconciling. Clebsch and Jaekle (1964), in their seminal work *Pastoral Care in Historical Perspective,* list these four functions as the key goals of pastoral care down through the ages. If you look closely at these words and their meanings, you will discover that they relate closely to all spiritual care work whether done in psychology or in religion. Presently, in our four steps of spiritual care, healing, sustaining, guiding, and reconciling follow directly as the four key long-term goals to our second step of the assessment of spiritual needs.

Healing aims to restore the person or community to some previous healthful state. This could be emotional or spiritual. Frequently, in spiritual assessment we ascertain that there is an area of a person's life that needs healing, such as overcoming fears and anxieties in a serious problem or illness. Usually when the word *healing* is used, we think of physical healing. This may be what we also pray and hope for; but in all cases in spiritual care, we are looking for the internal healing of a person's mind and spirit, that he or she be restored to a sure state of equilibrium and peace.

Sustaining aims to support the person as he or she endures a very difficult situation that will not be easily, if ever, resolved or eliminated. Our spiritual assessment may point out that the most important care we can bring is simply to stay with a person in his or her pains and struggles. Our sustaining efforts help the person to persevere. We offer empathy in painful situations and consolation at actual losses. When possible, we help the person regroup and find a foundation to continue to go on.

Guiding aims to provide assistance in making choices. What wisdom can the helpee draw upon to resolve difficult problems? Even if the problem is not solved, we know that we have really helped when we have listened well. The wisdom may indeed rise up within the helpee. At the other end of the continuum from listening is giving information and advice. We do this in a collaborative rather than a condescending way. Indeed spiritual assessment helps clarify and point out areas that need good guidance, leading to healthy choices and decisions.

Reconciling aims at restoring broken relationships between a person and another person, a community, with God, or even within the self. Spiritual assessment frequently points out the spiritual need to feel peace in one's heart, free from past painful experiences and resentments. The movement of reconciliation begins with the process of forgiveness of the other and/or the self. Beyond forgiveness, actual human connection and reconciliation with the other person may or may not take place depending on the issues and circumstances.

One of the advantages of using these four goals of spiritual care is that they increase our approaches and resources in responding to helpees' spiritual needs. They increase our creative imaginations in spiritually caring for others through four strategies, interventions, or ways of helping. Looking at these four goals of spiritual care within the framework of our present psychological culture, we would easily or might first choose the third way, the path of guiding another. For when we think of helping, we usually think of how we can lead and facilitate problem resolution or change of attitude in our helpees. However, step three of spiritual care, "determining the goals of spiritual care," points out that we can also help and care for others through healing, through simply sustaining them, and through leading them to reconciliation within themselves and with others. For example, we might now be even more aware that one of the key functions of spiritual care is to be with the helpee, thus sustaining his or her spirit. We do not always have to be doing for the other. This is especially true in situations such as bereavement, when we can do nothing. We simply need to facilitate that the other person can be in his or her pain and thus move through it. We model this process for them by simply being with them. This may be difficult for us as caregivers because we have to give up our power of doing for the other and rather help the other person find and experience more sustaining spiritual power within the self.

As you reflect on these four goals of spiritual care, which of the four do you think that people in the present-day most need? Clebsch and Jaekle (1964) state that in the centuries of the Christian era, each age has needed and usually focused on one particular goal of spiritual care. The past century, even until now, with its psychological focus and many human problems, has looked toward guidance to solve issues and problems. The first age of Christianity focused on sustaining the early Christians living and dying in horrifying times of repeated persecutions. In our present century, with its lack of community and scattered relationships, perhaps we now need more reconciliation and internal healing as the goals of spiritual care. What do you think should be the goals of spiritual care in regard to today's problems?

I very much like step three of our spiritual care model. I find that its four goals of spiritual care do for the caregiver what their terms designate. As the helper lives and facilitates the spiritual care of healing, sustaining, guiding, and reconciling with and to helpees, the same process marvelously takes place within the helper.

With regard to the two case studies, what goals of spiritual care would you ascertain for them? The elderly man is already experiencing strong spiritual well-being. He appears to be at peace and reconciled with family and friends, with his life and his destiny. However, spiritual well-being is always a process. The challenges of his growth continue. The elderly man faces the challenge of his dying. He will continue to need support to experience the four goals of spiritual care. Through continued spiritual care, hopefully he can find even deeper wisdom and peace to prepare for his death. Most of all he will need encouragement and the support of family and friends to sustain his courage and hope. Continued healing will come in his heart and spirit with such support, with prayer, and his hope in Christ. The woman with heart disease has more defined spiritual care goals. She still lives in fear because she does not feel really forgiven for her past misdeeds. Her spiritual care goals are further reconciliation with her God and the healing that this will bring to her soul and heart. She needs our guidance and sustaining presence to accomplish these goals.

Reflection Questions: Healing, sustaining, guiding, and reconciling are the goals of spiritual care. When you think of spirituality and spiritual care responses, can you think in regard to these long-term goals? Can you identify some specific strategies or techniques you can or do use to facilitate healing, sustaining, guiding, and reconciling with your helpees?

STEP FOUR: RELATE SPIRITUAL CARE
TO THE HELPEE'S RELIGION/BELIEFS

In this fourth step, we will examine two processes of assessment: (1) theological and (2) religious, making a distinction between them and looking at recent developments in both areas. For our purposes, in regard to spiritual assessment and care, we see theology as a person's beliefs in regard to God and/or transcendence. We view religion as an expression of relationship with God and/or transcendence through beliefs and practices lived out in a social institution (Ellwood, 1990).

For the helpee gifted with theological beliefs and/or a religion, we ask how might the helper assess and, if appropriate, effectively use them in the helping process of spiritual care. Pastoral care workers have always used a person's religion in their work. Traditional counselors and psychologists have until recently mostly ignored their helpees' religion. As we saw earlier, this happened and continues to occur because of Freud's view of religion as mostly pathology and our culture's view that religion is a very personal matter not to be discussed. Yet according to a Gallup poll, statistically over 90 percent of Americans say that they believe in God and over 65 percent say that religion is very important in their lives (Princeton Religious Research Center, 1993). Counselors who realize this are starting to question past practices and look to employ their helpees' theological beliefs/religion when applicable to their problems. If a person is healthily religious, why should that person not expect that his or her religious faith be respected, accepted, and even used for personal growth and change?

However, some helping professionals, because they lack the knowledge and competence, fear using their helpees' religion in the counseling process. This is changing as helping professionals become more familiar with and accepting of the multicultural expressions of their helpees, seeing religion as an important and even core cultural characteristic for many. Kelly (1995) states that religion is being seen by many counselors and social workers as an important psychosocial factor of clients' development. Further, Kelly explains how the counselor can use a person's religious concerns in counseling even if the counselor is not particularly religious or familiar with the helpee's particular religion. The helper can ask questions and learn about the helpee's religion. Through respect for the helpee, good listening, and inquiring about his or her religion, the counselor can clarify how religious beliefs relate to the client's concerns. When a person's religious faith gives strength, the counselor can help the client use it as a resource for change and growth. When a person's religion leads to guilt, whether healthy or unhealthy, the counselor does not downplay or ignore the helpee's religion, but works through it with him or her. A referral to a religious professional may especially be called for at this time. The theological beliefs/religious faith of the person are respected and made use of in psychological helping, leading to internal spiritual healing.

Theological Assessment

Several models have evolved to facilitate assessment of helpees' beliefs and theology. The best-known and most-used model is probably Paul Pruyser's (1976) seven theological belief themes. The helpee's life experience is viewed under the perspectives of the following:

1. Awareness of the Holy
2. Providence
3. Faith
4. Grace or Gracefulness
5. Repentance
6. Communion
7. Vocation

Based on our informal conversation model of spiritual assessment, the helper would reflect on the helpee's story in the light of these theological or life belief themes. Pruyser, as a psychologist in a hospital setting, felt disappointed that hospital chaplains in team meetings with other helping professionals did not use their theology in assessing patients. For the most part, they depended on a psychological model similar to social workers and psychologists. He encouraged chaplains to stop submerging their theological viewpoint. To accomplish this end, Pruyser developed the assessment model of seven theological themes. The chaplain would assess the patient's spiritual well-being in relation to these seven theological or life belief themes. For example, the chaplain would see patients with despair, with deep or shaken loyalty, with weak faith or disbelief, with loss of hope, etc. Seeing a religious patient in fear and distress, how might the chaplain call upon the resources of a person's theological beliefs? Could the chaplain in such a situation use the patient's awareness of the Holy (God), and sense of providence of a Higher Power? With a patient with wavering hope, could not the chaplain use the patient's past beliefs and faith?

Pruyser called attention to the fact that theological themes, whether they are doubts of faith in general or feelings of abandonment by

God, speak in experiential terms to patients' human dilemmas. Indeed, theological themes are functional perspectives and realities in helpees' lives, not just abstract terms. A person's theology, what he or she believes, certainly affects him or her emotionally and psychologically as well as spiritually. A sense of sin, an image of God, or a view of salvation influences a helpee's whole outlook on life and sense of well-being as a person. As such, theological assessments can indeed make a significant contribution toward whole-person care whether in psychology or in religion. Theological experiences and beliefs can be used in working toward psychological and spiritual healing and wholeness.

When you first view Pruyser's theological themes, you may object that you could never use theological language with your helpees. You may respond that you will remain with the simpler model of the four core areas of spiritual needs. Theological terms such as salvation, sin, and repentance would be too risky to use with your clients. Probably it would scare them off. True, many people do not connect with God-talk, such as repentance, grace, faith, and providence. The helper might well come across as a preacher and a proselytizer. Pruyser would most probably agree with you. He does not see the helping professional professing the faith or speaking theologically, so to speak, but rather using the helpee's religious practices and theological beliefs to reach a deeper meaningful spiritual level behind the person's theological beliefs in his or her life experience and concerns. Pruyser states that getting at this spiritual level does not usually mean outwardly employing theological language, God-talk with the helpee. Rather he states that on the part of the helper "what is needed is theological alertness" (1967, p. 63). This means that the helper reflects on the helpee's story in light of these theological themes. However, he or she restates these theological themes to the helpee in language that relates to his or her human experience.

Pruyser recommends a middle path with regard to theological terms. This middle path of helping is neither to speak psychologically to the helpee nor to directly speak theologically. For example, the psychologist usually does not speak literally psychologically to the helpee with terms such as psychosis, behavioral disorder, etc; nor need the spiritual care worker usually use explicit religious terms such as sin, salvation, grace, and redemption. In Pruyser's model the helper himself or herself reflects on how the helpee's theology or strongest beliefs influence and guide his or her life experience. For example, with the elderly man with terminal cancer, the helper knows of and reflects on the man's belief in Christ's suffering, death, and resurrection. However, to enable the elderly man to get in touch with the healing energies of this theological belief, the helper would relate this belief to human experience and language rather than simply use God-talk. For example, the helper might speak with him of a common life experience of "getting knocked down in life and getting back up again." How many countless times do we humans get knocked down and manage to rise again? The elderly man has been really knocked down with terminal cancer. Can he develop hope based on his previous life experiences of getting knocked down and getting up again and his present belief that as God has always brought him through past struggles, now God will be with him in his present terminal disease? God will pick him up and lead him through it. His theological belief in God's providence can give meaning and indeed can truly transform his dire situation. In sum, the helper, in responding to the helpee's theological belief of God's providence and care, uses language related more to human experience. In this case the language is "getting knocked down and getting back up again." Nonetheless, the helpee's healing theological belief can accurately be found there.

John Patton (1985), in his article "The New Language of Pastoral Counseling," sums it up this way: "An appropriate language in counseling for understanding and sharing experience is neither psychology nor theology, although it is psychological and theological. It is 'close-to-experience' language which is clinical, mediating, and relational" (p. 74). In the case study, the helper takes the narrative of the elderly man's life story, addresses in experiential language the belief themes in the story, and with their transforming effect moves him into and through his cancer toward the next chapter in his life. Even in the midst of active dying, people can find peace if they are able to draw upon the spirituality of their theological beliefs. The elderly man's theological beliefs give him the ability to turn his terminal cancer over to God. In effect, this gives him a wider perspective and a greater acceptance of his situation. His theological beliefs bring him meaning and purpose. They truly sustain him.

Theological Beliefs Expressed
in Experiential Spiritual Language

I would suggest that theological dimensions, expressed in the language of spirit or spirituality, are found in many human experiences. Whether nonreligious or religious, a person moving beyond self toward transcendence can experience Pruyser's theological themes in her or his life. For example, moving beyond self, one may have an experience of the holy in nature as well as in the practices of his or her religion. It is the spirit of the theological belief that gives meaning, and spiritual language draws out the richness of our theological and belief experiences. This spirit and spirituality is the middle path integrating psychological wholeness and religious healing. This holds true not only for the religious professionals but also for psychological professionals. Let us look now at Pruyser's theological themes in regard to this experiential spiritual middle path.

Theological Themes	Experiential Spiritual Language
Awareness of the Holy God as Holy. We are holy living with God.	What does he or she most revere, find sacred? The person's sense of awe and wonder?
Providence God cares for us. God's blessing of creation.	Does the person have anyone or anything that he or she depends on? Has he or she been blessed? How?
Faith Faith in God. Religious experiences.	Does the person have a sense of confidence in life? Does he or she embrace it or avoid it? What does he or she really believe in?
Grace or Gracefulness Need for God's grace and forgiveness. God smiles on.	For what does the person give thanks? Is he or she a self-made person or has he or she freely received from beyond self? When has the person needed forgiveness? Can the person forgive another who hurt him or her?

Theological Themes	Experiential Spiritual Language
Repentance	
All are sinners. Need for conversion, change of heart, salvation.	Does the person take responsibility for past wrongs, sins? What times of repentance has he or she been through? Is there any guilt?
Communion	
Union with God or a faith community.	Where is the person's community? How does he or she deal with loneliness? What are his or her deepest connections? Any feelings of shame from not being in union or belonging, etc.?
Vocation	
A sense of mission as part of God's plan. I am a significant and holy person in a divine plan.	Does the person have a sense of direction or deeper purpose in life? How does he or she want to look back on his or her life?

(Note: Some of these statements were developed from: Oates, 1982, pp. 185-186; Pruyser, 1976, pp. 60-79; Sackett, 1985, pp. 28-30.)

The helper may get the impression that doing a theological assessment is simply asking a series of questions. Pruyser emphatically did not want the chaplain to question the patient with one theme after the other. Rather he hoped that the chaplain would simply keep in mind his model of belief/theological themes as he or she conversed with the patient. From this process, the chaplain would later develop a "narrative" type of assessment about the patient that would illustrate and explain the patient's life experience in regard to his or her belief/theological perception. From this type of assessment, the chaplain could then respond and intervene with spiritual and psychological resources.

Reflection Questions: As a counselor or other psychological helper, could you envision bringing a person's theological or life beliefs into your helping process? If so, when might this be appropriate and how might you do it? Theology and theological terms are unfamiliar to many people. However, discuss or show how the spiritual meanings of these theological terms relate to most human life experiences and concerns. With these themes in mind, could you reflect spiritually or theologically on your clients? Could you do the same with yourself?

As an example of this theological narrative using spiritual language, let us return to the woman with the life-threatening heart disease and recap her story through Pruyser's seven theological themes.

Awareness of the Holy. In the helper's conversations with the woman, the woman frequently speaks of her awareness of a Higher Power who saves her from alcoholism. This Higher Power always remains with her. Throughout the day, she frequently talks with this Higher Power. She speaks of how she prays to God in the morning and at night, thanking God for keeping her from drinking that day. Certainly, she has a strong awareness of the Holy surrounding her. The helper could draw upon this sense of the Holy in working with the helpee.

Providence. However, in her present serious heart condition, she appears to have lost her sense of God's continuous providence and care. She speaks of how in her earlier years she learned that God was harsh and judgmental. In AA she encountered a more compassionate Higher Power. The helper finds, however, that in her present sickness and fears, the woman is now reverting to her old harsh image of God, wondering whether God will condemn her when she dies. Her theological narrative here informs us that she needs a stronger sense of providence in her present situation. The helper responds to this need for providence and care through the caring relationship that he or she continues with the woman. Out of the helper's loving care and reminders to her of her loving Higher Power, the helpee may come to know a more loving God of divine providence.

Faith. The helpee obviously believes in a Higher Power. This Higher Power has brought her back to a life of sobriety. She has a strong faith in her God even though she worries about God's judgment. Until her debilitating sickness, she was very involved in life. This life involvement shows her strong faith. She does not give up easily. This faith will help her face future fears and changes in her health.

Grace or Gracefulness. The woman certainly feels that she has been graced with many years of sobriety. She believes that her Higher Power has saved her. Also, she is very appreciative of the people caring for her in her sickness. She has a strong sense of gratitude for the many good moments of her life. If there is time, the helper could also explore and integrate with her the difficult times. In this way, she might also become aware of how the dark times, even personal failures, led to new life. With such support, she could expand even further her sense of gratitude, grace, and gracefulness.

Repentance. At the time that she completed the fourth step of AA, she listed her faults, failings, and sins. At that time also, she sought to make amends with the people that she had hurt in the past. She still expresses sorrow for the alcoholism that played a significant part in these past hurts. She has a remaining need to truly feel God's forgiveness for her past failings. Although she has repented and asked for others' and God's forgiveness, she does not feel completely forgiven by God. The helper needs to lead her to this forgiveness. By accepting her with her past failings and repentance, the helper shows the woman the forgiveness and acceptance of God. The helper might also develop a healing ritual or visual imagery with the theme of God's forgiveness. He or she might call upon a religious professional to lead a healing ritual of forgiveness from the helpee's faith tradition.

Communion. The woman lives in a spirit of communion and community, closely connected with her AA friends. The helper observes how not just medical staff but friends and relatives are really caring for her in her present pains and needs, just as she has reached out to them over the years. She is not a person in isolation. Community surrounds her, and the helper senses that it is part of her very spirit as a person. Although she is in strong communion with those around her, she still struggles to experience stronger forgiveness and closer communion with her God.

Vocation. Finally, with regard to her vocation or more precisely her present purpose or calling in life, she faces life with uncertainty and fear. She fears the death that seems to be quickly approaching from her debilitating heart disease. Many people say that they are not afraid of death itself as much as they fear the final process it takes to get there. She fears both: death itself and the possibility of enduring even stronger pain before she dies. What might her theological belief in a Higher Power who saved her from her alcoholism say to her about her present purpose in life? What is a deeper calling for her at this time?

From reviewing this woman's theological narrative and reflecting on its life belief themes, the helper assesses that she most needs healing and guidance in the areas of repentance, forgiveness, and her present purpose in life. The helper accepts the woman with her pains and fears. If it is possible, the helper needs to facilitate the woman in reframing her difficult situation in the light of her spiritual values and relationship with a loving Higher Power. This loving Higher Power brought life out of her past struggles. Can her Higher Power sustain her now? The helper, however, notes that at this point the woman has become too weak to talk for more than about five minutes at a time. Her heart is weakening, and she is overwhelmed with exhaustion. The helper's spiritual care will now center more on using ritual care through praying words of forgiveness with her, asking for freedom from fear, and a fullness of peace. Also the helper may read prayers of healing from a favorite AA prayer book that is always by the woman's side. Mostly, the helper will sit silently with the woman, offering her courage and complete acceptance.

Through this theological assessment of the woman's story, can we see how theological perceptions and life beliefs affect a person's psychological and spiritual health? Theological themes, a person's beliefs, are deep experiences of life. Theological themes are not so much substantive issues to be debated and discussed as much as they are functional elements lived in human psychological and spiritual experiences. Through developing a middle path of spiritual language in a narrative between psychology and theology, we as helpers can better facilitate healing and wholeness.

Practical Exercise

Choose either yourself or a helpee, and out of a specific concern or issue, develop a theological/spiritual narrative. Look at the key theological themes and conflicts of the person's narrative, identifying possible spiritual strategies for healing and well-being.

Explicit Religious Assessment

Malony (1996) has developed a model of religious assessment that employs explicit religious language in working with helpees who actively live their beliefs through a religious tradition. He disagrees with Pruyser who, as we saw, shies away from religious language even with clients who consider themselves religious. Malony believes that one of the main goals of counseling is to help clients adjust to their environments. If their religion is important to them, then helping clients adjust to and even grow into their religious environments is a normal part of counseling. If we state that our care is person-centered, then we need to respond to what is important to each person. If religion and religious terminology are important to the client, the counselor should be able to empathize with and use some basic religious language. To accomplish these objectives, Malony (1988, 1994) developed what he terms the religious status interview or religious status inventory. In this religious assessment tool, he takes Pruyser's seven theological themes and develops eight themes with specific questions related to religion. Similar to Pruyser, he notes that these questions do not so much focus on the substance of belief or dogma, but rather on the functional aspects of a person's religion, how the tenets or practices of a person's religion relate to his or her concerns and present psychological and spiritual growth. The following are typical questions taken from his religious status interview:

1. Awareness of God

   Who or what is God to you?
   In your day-to-day life, for which things do you depend upon God and for which things do you not?
   In what situations do you pray to God?

2. Acceptance of God's Grace and Steadfast Love

   How does God respond to you when you sin?
   How do you respond to God's love and forgiveness?
   Why do you think God allows personal suffering in your life?

3. Being Repentant and Responsible

   How do you feel and respond when you have wronged someone?
   What do you do when you have wronged someone?
   When someone has wronged you, how do you respond to him or her?

4. Knowing God's Leadership and Direction

How do you make major decisions in your life?
How is your faith related to your various roles in your family, occupation, and community?

5. Involvement in Organized Religion

How often do you attend the activities of your church or religious community?
Why do you attend church?

6. Experiencing Fellowship

Tell me about your relationships with other people, both Christians and non-Christians.
What does being part of the body of believers mean to you?

7. Being Ethical

How do you decide what is right and wrong?
How does your faith influence your sense of what is right and wrong?
What ethical issues are you concerned about and how do you deal with them?

8. Affirming Openness in Faith

How does your faith affect different parts of your life?
Tell me about the dimensions, or parts, of your faith that are important to you. (Selections taken from "The Clinical Assessment of Religious Functioning" by H. Newton Malony, 1988. *Review of Religious Research, 30,* pp. 8-11. Reprinted by permission.)

Malony's religious assessment comes out of a Christian context. However, his hope and feeling are that a helper could freely adjust the questions to other religious traditions. Note, however, that its focus is that of a more evangelical context. A more sacramentally focused Christian church, such as the Catholic or Orthodox or Episcopalian, might add a sacramental focus to Malony's religious assessment. The following questions model such a sacramental path with a spiritual care focus.

Sacramentally Focused Religious Assessment*

Sacramental Assessment	Experiential Spiritual Path
Baptism (Dignity as spiritual need)	Do you feel accepted as a child of God? How does this situation affect your self-image?
Confirmation (Power as spiritual need)	In which areas of your life do you feel that you have the most control or influence? What strength does your faith give you in making choices for your life?
Sacrament of Ordination (Meaning as spiritual need)	How has this situation or illness changed your meaning or calling?
(Calling as spiritual need)	To what purpose or direction do you feel called by God?
Eucharist (Celebration as spiritual need)	How do you celebrate your life? Where do you find hope in everyday life? What wisdom or truth do you find living in your situation?
Reconciliation (Freedom as spiritual need)	In what ways does your faith help you make peace with your regrets or guilt? How are you feeling about the life you have lived up to now?
Marriage (Relationship as spiritual need)	What relationships in your life are most important? How would you describe your own relationship with God? How has this situation changed your relationships?

Reflection Questions: Many psychological helpers disagree or at least use extreme caution in using religious language in their work. Why might this be so? What do you think? Do you agree or disagree

---

*This section is based on a presentation by the late Rev. Susan Lyons, Hartford Hospital, Hartford, Connecticut.

with Malony's position that with a helpee to whom religion is an important way of life, a helping professional should be open to using religious language? As a religious professional do you use or how do you use religious language with your helpees? Can you restate or reframe religious language in more spiritual-type language?

CONCLUSION

The reader may have concluded that these models of spiritual, theological, and religious assessment are too involved and complicated to use practically. The reader may think that there are too many ideas or pieces to keep track of and bring together. I have purposefully provided an expanded view of spiritual assessment and care. This detailed view shows the many possibilities of integrating spirituality and spiritual needs more fully into psychology and theology. Spiritual assessment and care are parts of both the psychosocial and the religious perspective of the person.

However, the best way to learn spiritual assessment is simply to begin to do it in an uncomplicated way. The models of theological and religious assessment are for more developed reflection, learning, and action. For example, as I talk with a helpee, I simply begin to reflect on his or her story through using the beginning model of the four core spiritual needs. Spiritual care and assessment are intentional processes. For myself I activate this intentional process through the "Take Five Approach." I take five minutes of quiet time and write down some initial reactions I have to the client in regard to the four spiritual needs: meaning, giving love, receiving love, forgiveness and hope. I list the four words or spiritual needs on a piece of paper and fill in observations under each word. I find this informal process very moving and enlightening. In fact, this may be all that you want or need to do for a particular spiritual assessment.

Just doing this first step of a brief spiritual assessment enables the helper to empathize with the helpee's concerns and spiritual needs. This process often enables the helper to become aware of the helpee's psychological, spiritual, and religious strengths that have not been previously evident. For example, after talking with the elderly man, our earlier example, the helper might wondrously experience how someone whose spiritual needs are fulfilled can face even death. It can be quite an experience for the helper to observe this. Doing an intentional spiritual assessment, even a brief one, enables the helper to see how spirituality integrates and completes the helpee's psychological and religious needs. Spirituality will become for the helper a striking reality in human assessment and life. It will no longer be an abstract concept. Doing this simple first step of spiritual assessment will enable the helper to feel more at ease in working with a person's spirituality. As a consequence, it can also lead the helper to be more involved in her or his own spiritual processes. Finally, doing a simple spiritual assessment will bring up further suggestions and questions on how to work with the helpee. When a spiritual need is lacking, how does the helper reach out with spiritual care to this need?

After completing the first step of the assessment of spiritual needs, the helper can decide when and how to use the last two steps of the model: determining the long-term goal of spiritual care and relating spiritual care to the helpee's religion/beliefs. As a religious professional, I have found the theological assessment very helpful to work with. To my surprise, I have found Pruyser's theological themes also very applicable for nonreligious helpees. My experience is that everyone, religious and nonreligious, has beliefs regarding these life themes that they function out of. Kathleen Norris (1998), in her popular book *Amazing Grace: A Vocabulary of Faith,* effectively shows how theological concepts are part of everyone's world. Regardless, the point is helpers need to take the first step of doing spiritual assessment. Begin. Take five minutes. You may find this first step sufficient. You may move on to further surprisingly sturdy steps of spiritual assessment, care, and growth.

Chapter 4

Tools for Spiritual Assessment:
Spiritual Care As a Clinical Science

In this chapter, several standardized spiritual assessment instruments will be examined. We will also study several developmental models of spiritual growth from a spiritual assessment viewpoint, and learn how to do a spiritual assessment by conducting a semi-structured interview while using a survey instrument. From Chapter 3 we are familiar with what we termed an "informal" process of spiritual assessment, that is, an assessment done without an assessment survey or a developed instrument. In informal assessment, we get to know the helpee better from a spiritual perspective through conversation. However, presently many helping professionals and their organizations are looking for a more formal spiritual assessment tool. They desire to use already-developed instruments or to draw up new survey assessment tools for their particular settings.

THE NEED FOR SPIRITUAL ASSESSMENT INSTRUMENTS

Why is there a need for formal spiritual assessment instruments, if a spiritual assessment can be informally accomplished through identifying spiritual needs in a conversation with a helpee? First, using a spiritual assessment instrument or survey can make spiritual care more real and more concrete both for the helpee and the helper. It moves spiritual assessment out of the background and into focus, and can facilitate improved decision making with regard to spiritual needs and growth. At the least, spiritual assessment instruments jump-start the helpee's needed self-reflection regarding his or her spiritual needs. They clearly and concretely point out directions for spiritual healing and growth opportunities.

Second, better spiritual care can happen more quickly as a result of spiritual assessment instruments. Spiritual caregivers, with the information taken from an instrument or survey about helpees' spiritual and religious needs and conditions, will have both a broader and at the same time a more precise picture of the helpees that they are working with. With more information about the whole person, they will have a better feel for helpees' struggles and concerns and as a result grow in empathy and understanding for them.

Third, spiritual assessment instruments and surveys enhance spiritual caregivers' status as contributing professional members of their organizations. Teams of professionals using a spiritual assessment survey more directly and easily bring credibility to spirituality in their work settings. Some administrators may question the value of spiritual care work, but a survey enables these helpers to clinically measure and show their work effectiveness with clients' spiritual needs. Moreover, through the use of a survey form or instrument, spiritual caregivers can share feedback and learn from each other. Through documented results of spiritual assessments, better coordination will take place among them resulting in better holistic client care.

Fourth, use of instruments and surveys by spiritual caregivers will bring them more acceptance from other professionals outside their field. The documented spiritual information that they chart from instruments and surveys will enable the entire field of spiritual care to become better known. As spiritual needs are documented for various health conditions and personality issues, all professional helpers will become more aware that these needs are important for the total well-being of a person. Interventions can be determined for specific spiritual problems and needs.

For example, for several years hospital chaplains have been using spiritual assessment instruments to evaluate the impact of spiritual care on patients' physical and psychological health. They have looked at questions such as the possible therapeutic effects of intercessory prayer on patients' physical health and the role of spiritual beliefs in dealing with depression (VandeCreek, 1995). Through documentation, chaplains have also shown that spiritual care effectively serves the financial necessities of a hospital. Helpers can use this documented information to seek funding for spiritual care and research. In one study, orthopedic patients who received spiritual care spent less time in the hospital and needed significantly less pain medication than those who did not receive spiritual care (Florell in McSherry, 1987a).

In sum, instruments and surveys of spiritual assessment facilitate clarity, importance, and more acceptance of the effectiveness of spiritual assessment and care.

STUMBLING BLOCKS TO SPIRITUAL ASSESSMENT

Despite the previous reasons, some spiritual caregivers are fearfully averse to using formal spiritual assessment instruments. They feel these instruments could impede and even hurt the helping relationship, and fear that the warmth, spontaneity, and closeness of this relationship could be compromised if the helper uses a survey instrument. The helpee might feel that he or she is the subject of an experiment or a research study. Surveys with structured interviews and formal instruments could be too intrusive. Stoddard and Burns-Haney (1990), in "Developing an Integrated Approach to Spiritual Assessment," even rate types of assessment tools according to how intrusive they might be. They speak of assessment surveys and instruments as "more intrusive" than other methods of spiritual assessment such as the semistructured interview, which they see as "somewhat less intrusive," and the pastoral or spiritual conversation as the "least intrusive" (pp. 78-79). They state that only the more advanced helpers should use formal instruments with their helpees. Helpers need to be familiar with the instruments and have the sensitivity to use them in a nonthreatening way.

In contrast, Elizabeth McSherry (1987b) points out that frequently the negative feeling over spiritual assessment forms and instruments is simply from the "fear of change" (p. 10). She believes that as the helper uses an instrument or survey, not only will the helper experience its effectiveness for the helpee, but may hear the helpee's grateful "thank you" for bringing to light his or her spiritual needs through the assessment instrument. Effective spiritual care can no longer be merely following intuition in a friendly conversation, but rather a real practice of observing identifiable spiritual needs, concerns, and opportunities. McSherry calls the helper's observation of spiritual needs a "clinical science" with a language and "practice method" of its own (p. 1).

Indeed, in most cases spiritual assessment instruments are very useful. They clinically help identify spiritual needs for a helpee who desires further spiritual growth. They aid the helper who sees a need for a particular helpee to clearly identify unknown areas of spiritual need. In short, spiritual assessment tools can facilitate expanded personal knowledge about a person's spiritual needs, maturity, and well-being. McSherry hopes that any present aversion to spiritual assessment instruments is not unwillingness on the helper's part to be more explicit and thorough about spiritual care. Spiritual assessment instruments can give helpers more knowledge and competency in areas of spiritual needs and growth. As a result, spiritual caregivers can then respond to these spiritual needs with specific interventions. To accomplish this goal, we will review several of these instruments.

Reflection Questions: Do you see value in using a survey form or an instrument of spiritual assessment to assess spiritual needs? Would you prefer to do a more informal spiritual assessment through a listening conversation? State the pros and cons of each method. How do you think that spirituality can be more accepted professionally in all helping fields? Is the ability to do a spiritual assessment part of this process?

CLINICAL INSTRUMENTS OF SPIRITUAL ASSESSMENT

Spiritual Well-Being Scale

One of the first instruments and certainly the one that researchers have most used is Paloutzian and Ellison's (1991) spiritual well-being scale (Figure 4.1). For more than two decades these two researchers have sought to determine more precisely the characteristics of spiritual well-being (Paloutzian and Ellison, 1980; Ellison, 1983). They base their view of spiritual well-being on its definition from the 1975 National Interfaith Coalition on Aging. "Spiritual well-being is the affirmation of life in a relationship with God, self, community and environment that nurtures and celebrates wholeness" (p. 1). From this definition they conclude that we as humans find wholeness in two ways: by seeking transcendence beyond ourselves and by satisfying

For each of the following statements, circle the choice that best indicates the extent of your agreement or disagreement as it describes your personal experience:

SA = Strongly Agree	D = Disagree
MA = Moderately Agree	MD = Moderately Disagree
A = Agree	SD = Strongly Disagree

1. I don't find much satisfaction in private prayer with God.	SA	MA	A	D	MD	SD
2. I don't know who I am, where I came from, or where I'm going.	SA	MA	A	D	MD	SD
3. I believe that God loves me and cares about me.	SA	MA	A	D	MD	SD
4. I feel that life is a positive experience.	SA	MA	A	D	MD	SD
5. I believe that God is impersonal and not interested in my daily situations.	SA	MA	A	D	MD	SD
6. I feel unsettled about my future.	SA	MA	A	D	MD	SD
7. I have a personally meaningful relationship with God.	SA	MA	A	D	MD	SD
8. I feel very fulfilled and satisfied with life.	SA	MA	A	D	MD	SD
9. I don't get much personal strength and support from my God.	SA	MA	A	D	MD	SD
10. I feel a sense of well-being about the direction my life is headed in.	SA	MA	A	D	MD	SD
11. I believe that God is concerned about my problems.	SA	MA	A	D	MD	SD
12 I don't enjoy much about life.	SA	MA	A	D	MD	SD
13. I don't have a personally satisfying relationship with God.	SA	MA	A	D	MD	SD
14. I feel good about my future.	SA	MA	A	D	MD	SD
15. My relationship with God helps me not to feel lonely.	SA	MA	A	D	MD	SD
16. I feel that life is full of conflict and unhappiness.	SA	MA	A	D	MD	SD
17. I feel most fulfilled when I'm in close communion with God.	SA	MA	A	D	MD	SD
18. Life doesn't have much meaning.	SA	MA	A	D	MD	SD
19. My relationship with God contributes to my sense of well-being.	SA	MA	A	D	MD	SD
20. I believe there is some real purpose for my life.	SA	MA	A	D	MD	SD

Note: Items are scored from 1 to 6, with a higher number representing more well-being. Reverse scoring for negatively worded items. Odd-numbered items assess religious well-being; even-numbered items assess existential well-being.

FIGURE 4.1. Spiritual Well-Being Scale (*Source:* SWB Scale Copyright © 1982 by Craig W. Ellison and Raymond F. Paloutzian. All rights reserved. Not to be duplicated unless express written permission is granted by the authors or by Life Advance, Inc., 81 Front St., Nyack, NY 10960. Reprinted by permission.)

our needs for having, relating, and being self-fulfilled. They call these two ways the vertical and the horizontal components of being human. The vertical or transcendent is our relationship with God; the horizontal or existential is our relationship to our own sense of life purpose, meaning, and life satisfactions. After completing the instrument, a person receives a score for the vertical or religious sense of well-being and the horizontal or existential sense of well-being. The combination of the two scores is a person's total score of spiritual well-being.

After the completion and scoring of this short instrument, the helper asks the helpee if he or she agrees with the results. As with any assessment instrument, it is only valid for the helpee if he or she sees the results in himself or herself. If the helpee does not relate to the results, the helper generally should stay with the thinking of the helpee rather than that of the assessment instrument. If the helpee says, "Yes, this is me" or "This tells me something about myself," then the helper or counselor would encourage him or her to discuss some statements that stand out significantly. For example, the helpee may have agreed with the statement about life not having much meaning. This statement could be a launching pad to deeper exploration of a time when life had meaning or the helper could simply feel and explore with the helpee his or her experience of not finding meaning in life at this time. Based on the responses to the various statements, the helper works with the helpee's identified spiritual needs to set up goals leading to spiritual growth and ultimately stronger spiritual well-being.

Spiritual Health Inventory (SHI)

Since its questions are more generic, another instrument, the spiritual health inventory (SHI), may be more useful in diverse counseling situations (Kelly, 1995) (Figure 4.2). Veach and Chappel (1992) show in this instrument that spiritual health can be assessed without specifically inquiring about a person's image of God or participation in an organized religion. To accomplish this, they assess four areas of spirituality: (1) personal spiritual experience; (2) spiritual well-being that can result from "an active relationship with a higher power" (p. 145); (3) a sense of harmony that can arise from spiritual experience and spiritual well-being; and (4) an examination of personal

For each of the following statements, circle the choice that best indicates the extent of your agreement or disagreement.

SA = Strongly Agree	D = Disagree
MA= Moderately Agree	MD=Moderately Disagree
A = Agree	SD = Strongly Disagree

1. I have a sense of internal support or strength in dealing with illness or other problems.   SA MA A D MD SD

2. I experience a sense of harmony with the world and the universe as they exist.   SA MA A D MD SD

3. I believe in God, a Creator, or a Higher Power.   SA MA A D MD SD

4. God, the Creator, or Higher Power is so powerful that nothing I do makes any difference.   SA MA A D MD SD

5. I believe my life has meaning.   SA MA A D MD SD

6. It is my experience that developing and maintaining spiritual health requires effort and work.   SA MA A D MD SD

7. I *do not* believe that anything can be done to develop spiritual health.   SA MA A D MD SD

8. I have an internal experience of being accepted for who I am.   SA MA A D MD SD

9. I *do not* pray to God, a Creator, or a Higher Power.   SA MA A D MD SD

10. I believe my life has purpose.   SA MA A D MD SD

11. I experience the presence of God, the Creator, or Higher Power in my life.   SA MA A D MD SD

12. I have *no* experience of peace with myself or with others.   SA MA A D MD SD

13. I believe that God, the Creator, or my Higher Power will do things for me or to me.   SA MA A D MD SD

14. I have had a spiritual experience or a sense of spiritual awakening.   SA MA A D MD SD

15. I experience a sense of awe when I consider life and the universe.   SA MA A D MD SD

16. I *do not* believe there is such a thing as spiritual health.   SA MA A D MD SD

17. My experience of God, the Creator, or Higher Power leaves me with a sense of humility.   SA MA A D MD SD

18. I am grateful for all I have received from life.   SA MA A D MD SD

FIGURE 4.2. Spiritual Health Inventory (SHI) (*Source:* Tracy L. Veach and John N. Chappel, 1992. "Measuring Spiritual Health: A Preliminary Study." *Substance Abuse, 13,* 142-143. Reprinted by permission.)

helplessness, a term that the authors state needs more clarity. They see spiritual health as "essentially an internal experience of connection with some 'higher power': God, the Creator, Nature. It can be conceived of as linking into the 'Mind of the Universe'" (p. 141). As with the previous spiritual well-being scale, I also find this instrument useful in working with people who want to identify their spiritual needs and to develop specific areas of spiritual growth. For instance, a young man in completing this instrument checked that he did not see and experience his Higher Power or God as actively involved in his life. He became aware that although he saw himself relating to his God, he did not experience God's presence as a close relationship. He met God only at a distance. He asked, "How can I experience God as close and active in my life?" The SHI made him aware of this spiritual need.

INSPIRIT (Index of Core Spiritual Experiences)

In contrast to working with the young man whose God is distant, I have found INSPIRIT, the Index of Core Spiritual Experiences (see Figure 4.3) (Kass et al., 1991), a very useful instrument in working with those who have had a close experience of God—or other spiritual experiences. Typically, spiritual experiences such as divine energy or presence are often outrightly rebuffed by the helpee. They are feared as strange, and are felt once and then too quickly pushed aside and forgotten. INSPIRIT challenges this practice, seeing religious and spiritual experiences as opportunities leading to healthy intrinsic religiosity and spiritual support and growth. In order to facilitate stronger spiritual well-being, helpers need to teach helpees to be more aware of their spiritual and religious experiences and to draw upon them for courage and strength throughout their lives. INSPIRIT does this through the questions it asks the helpee. For example, question seven, asking for a description of a spiritual experience, enables a helpee to closely identify what happened in such an experience and what it might presently mean.

A spiritual or religious experience, once identified, shared with, and even celebrated with the helper, will frequently become a deep value in the helpee's life. As such, he or she will be able to draw upon this spiritual experience for energy and meaning in difficult times. A helpee shared an experience of a time when she was in complete

Instructions:

The following questions concern your spiritual or religious beliefs and experiences. There are no right or wrong answers. For each question, circle the number of the answer that is most true for you.

1. How strongly religious (or spiritually oriented) do you consider yourself to be? (strong; somewhat strong; not very strong; not at all; can't answer)

2. About how often do you spend time on religious or spiritual practices? (several times per day—several times per week; once per week—several times per month; once per month—several times per year; once a year or less)

3. How often have you felt as though you were very close to a powerful spiritual force that seemed to lift you outside yourself? (never; once or twice; several times; often; can't answer)

People have many different definitions of the "Higher Power" that we often call "God." Please use your definition of God when answering the following questions.

4. How close do you feel to God? (extremely close; somewhat close; not very close; I don't believe in God; can't answer)

5. Have you ever had an experience that has convinced you that God exists? (yes; no; can't answer)

6. Indicate whether you agree or disagree with this statement: "God dwells within you." (definitely disagree; tend to disagree; tend to agree; definitely agree)

7. The following list describes spiritual experiences that some people have had. Please indicate if you have had any of these experiences and the extent to which each of them has affected your belief in God.

The response choices are:

    I had this experience and it:
    4) Convinced me of God's existence;
    3) Strengthened belief in God; or
    2) Did not strengthen belief in God.
    1) I have never had this experience.

A. An experience of God's energy or presence
B. An experience of a great spiritual figure (e.g., Jesus, Mary, Elijah, Buddha)
C. An experience of angels or guiding spirits
D. An experience of communication with someone who has died
E. Meeting or listening to a spiritual teacher or master
F. An overwhelming experience of love
G. An experience of profound inner peace
H. An experience of complete joy and ecstasy
I. A miraculous (or not normally occurring) event
J. A healing of your body or mind (or witnessed such a healing)
K. A feeling of unity with the earth and all living beings
L. An experience with near death or life after death
M. Other _____

FIGURE 4.3. INSPIRIT Survey (*Source:* Jared D. Kass, Richard Friedman, Jane Leserman, Patricia C. Zuttermeister, and Herbert Benson, 1991, "Health Outcomes and a New Index of Spiritual Experience." *Journal for the Scientific Study of Religion, 30,* 210-211. Reprinted by permission.)

doubt about living up to a life of the Spirit. Yet following this doubt and despair, she had an overwhelming experience of God's energy and voice telling her that she was indeed already living a strong life of the Spirit. From that time on, she doubted herself less and moved through life with much more confidence and a spirit of love. She could always return to this religious/spiritual experience when in doubt. As you can see from this example, INSPIRIT is not only useful for spiritual assessment but it is also an effective resource to lead the helpee to further spiritual self-understanding, encouragement, and growth.

As an added note, VandeCreek, Ayres, and Bassham (1995) recommend that hospital chaplains leave INSPIRIT with helpees at the time of an initial visit to be completed and at a later time discussed with the chaplain. Especially the opening questions of INSPIRIT challenge the person to begin to reflect on his or her spirituality, asking how religious or spiritual the person sees himself or herself. One or two of INSPIRIT's questions, for example, would be very helpful in an intake interview for a counseling or other professional-help type setting.

Reflection Questions: Would you consider using any of the previous three instruments of spiritual assessment for your particular helping setting? Which do you think would be the most useful? Has surveying these instruments made spirituality more real and concrete for you? How might these instruments expand a person's vision of spirituality? What personal spiritual needs or possible growth areas have you discovered through completing these instruments? Has the INSPIRIT instrument made you more aware or given you any ideas on how to use a helpee's past spiritual/religious experience toward spiritual growth?

DEVELOPMENTAL MODELS
OF SPIRITUAL ASSESSMENT

Several models of spiritual assessment connect stages of spiritual growth with well-known psychological stages of human development. They relate spiritual stages of growth to psychological stages of maturity. In these developmental models of spirituality, the helper can determine the specific stage or level of the helpee's faith or spirituality in regard to his or her psychological stage of development. In these stage-step models, spiritual growth typically begins in childhood with a self-centered focus—that is, a spirituality or belief centered on a person's own spiritual needs and progresses into adulthood to a movement beyond self-interest to a spirituality or belief that is surpassing, transcending, and transformative. As an example, Capps (1979) takes Pruyser's eight theological life themes that we discussed in Chapter 3 and relates them to the psychologist Erik Erikson's eight human developmental stages of life. The counselor, doing a spiritual assessment, can use Erikson's model to determine the appropriate psychosocial life stage of the helpee and relate that stage to the ideal corresponding theological/spiritual focus of growth according to Pruyser's model.

For example, the theological theme of providence or sense of care in human life ideally develops at the earliest human development stage, which is Erikson's stage of trust versus mistrust. This is a time when a young child needs to develop trust in his or her parents and a resultant trust in life itself. If the child develops a sense of mistrust, this will influence his or her later spiritual growth as well as psychological life. He or she will always strive to overcome this early sense of mistrusting life and have a difficult time growing into a sense of God's care and providence. If a person cannot humanly trust another, how can he or she learn to trust in God's providence? As another example, the theological theme of "awareness of the Holy" occurs in the second half of life, as the person strives psychologically for a sense of integrity rather than despair. A person can develop a stronger sense of integrity through a theology or spirituality of awareness of the Holy. Awareness of God's presence in a person's life gives it deeper meaning. A person's life has progressed, as it should, with divine meaning.

Psychological and Theological Development

Also, Capps (1979) shows how theological themes can be used in pastoral counseling because the "structure of communication is theological" in pastoral counseling (p. 136). The following themes are adapted from Capps (1979, p. 114) and are reproduced with permission:

Pruyser's Theological Themes	Erikson's Psychosocial Themes
1. Providence	Trust versus mistrust
2. Grace or gracefulness	Autonomy versus shame and self-doubt
3. Repentance	Initiative versus guilt
4. Vocation	Industry versus inferiority
5. Faith	Identity versus identity diffusion
6. Communion	Intimacy versus isolation
7. Vocation	Generativity versus stagnation
8. Awareness of the Holy	Integrity versus despair

Can you see how the counselor could use this model in spiritually assessing clients at different stages of human growth and life? Moreover, for a religiously focused client, the counselor could draw upon a theological theme to strengthen a psychologically weak area. For example, with an adolescent or adult who has fear and mistrust both of self and of life, the counselor could help develop the client's belief in the love and trust of God. Helping usually moves from the psychological to the spiritual. However, the theological and spiritual can also strengthen the psychological. In this regard, the counselor could draw upon the scriptures for a quote or phrase of trusting in God that the client, when fearful, could frequently repeat. Such a phrase might be "And know that I am with you always; yes, to the end of time" (Matthew 28: 20). This process enables the client to name the mistrust and thus transform it through a spiritual process leading to the beginning of trust.

When working with a religiously oriented client, the counselor or helper could listen to the kinds of stories and examples that the helpee shares and relate them to theological/spiritual themes. If the helpee is always complaining about how hard he or she works with no appreciation from others, issues that perhaps center around Erikson's developmental stage of industry versus inferiority, the helper might focus on the possible theological or spiritual sense of meaning or vocation that a person finds in his or her work. In essence, Capps' developmental model shows that psychological growth and maturity can be closely related to spiritual development and well-being. Likewise, spiritual growth and maturity can lead to stronger psychological health.

Pastoral (Spiritual) Assessment

In another developmental model, Ivy (1987) describes and explains Fowler's (1981) stages of faith as stages of spiritual growth and consciousness. For Fowler, faith is not so much theological belief but rather a psychological outlook explained as the structural ways that humans find meaning. A person's faith is his or her meaning system. At different growth stages of human development, people find and structure their faith or meaning system in differing ways. Ivy takes Fowler's stages of faith or meaning and describes them more fully as stages of spiritual consciousness. Moreover, significantly for our spiritual care purposes, Ivy recommends various spiritual care interventions for each level of faith/spiritual consciousness. He firmly believes that "pastoral [spiritual] intervention should follow pastoral [spiritual] assessment" (1987, p. 338). Look now at Fowler's stages of faith or meaning development in relationship to Ivy's stages of spiritual consciousness. After discussing Fowler's stages of faith development in regard to Ivy's stages of spiritual development, some of Ivy's spiritual interventions for some of the stages will be shared.

The following lists are adapted from Ivy (1987, p. 335) and are reproduced with permission:

Fowler's Faith Development	**Ivy's Spiritual Consciousness**
1. Primal faith	Pleasure
2. Intuitive-projective faith	Magical
3. Mythic-literal faith	Literalizing
4. Synthetic-conventional faith	Interpersonal
5. Individuative-reflective faith	Idealizing/reflective
6. Conjunctive faith	Integrative
7. Universalizing faith	Unitive

Fowler (1990) identifies seven stages of faith development. (1) The earliest stage of faith development to age two, *primal faith,* originates in the child's interactions with the parents in which the child learns to face life with trust or mistrust. Ivy (1987) states that meaning or spiritual/religious consciousness for the child at this stage is *pleasure.* This spiritual consciousness develops from the child's experiencing life through feeling pleasure from the parents' acceptance, warmth, and love. (2) *Intuitive-projective faith,* ages two to six, arises when the child intuits the family's images of life and how they influence his or her existence. Spiritual/religious consciousness at this stage is *magical.* It grows from the child's feelings for the images and stories he or she hears and the fantasies and further images arising out of his or her magical consciousness. (3) *Mythic-literal faith,* ages seven to twelve, happens when the child really incorporates stories or narratives of the clan into self whether they be ethnic, racial, class, or religious. However, the meaning of these stories or spiritual/religious consciousness is one dimensional or *literal.* (4) *Synthetic-conventional faith* occurs around age twelve and takes place when the young person, drawing on the multidimensional images of the group, develops an identity of meaning as his or her own person in the group. His or her spiritual/religious consciousness is *interpersonal* coming from the beliefs and values of this primary group. The person at this stage looks for the conventional acceptance of peers. (5) *Individuative-reflective faith,* arising possibly between ages seventeen to twenty, comes with more maturity and with the possibility for self-reflection, awareness, and a person's acceptance of his or her individual difference and uniqueness. Internal conflict arises between the self and the group. Spiritual/religious consciousness at this level is *idealizing/reflective.* It is a thrust for reflection and finding true meaning within oneself and not only receiving meaning from others. (6) *Conjunctive faith,* possible after age thirty-five, comes from the person's need to rejoin the opposites and paradoxes of life. How does he or she make sense of a life that is frequently ambiguous at its best? Life is definitely no longer one dimensional or conventional only including self in clearly defined terms. One now transcends self-interests. At this stage, spiritual/religious consciousness is *integrative,* reaching out to find meaning in many beliefs and systems, not only a person's own chosen spiritual or religious path. (7) *Universalizing faith* comes when a person finds internal unity in the ground of being. What is the deeper common reality below the many meanings in the universe? How does a person not so much find these meanings but transparently become them? He or she stands open to all persons and all reality. At this stage the person's spiritual/religious consciousness is *unitive.* He or she seeks intimacy and finds meaning in being itself, that is being beyond himself or herself and in the very ground of being.

As was previously stated, Ivy (1987) not only explains Fowler's stages of faith in regard to spiritual development, he also develops specific spiritual care interventions to effectively strengthen and increase the level of spiritual consciousness. Using these interventions, the spiritual caregiver can work with the helpee at each level of faith development or spiritual consciousness. For instance, in the earliest stages of faith development when a person's meaning comes only from his or her primary caregivers, Ivy recommends that the caregiver encourage parents to be strongly invested in and dedicated to their children. From their relationship with their child at this stage, parents facilitate a basic feeling of what is meaningful for the child. At the later literalizing stage, the parent or the helper could use dramatic stories with the child that show the difference between good and evil. At the idealizing and reflective stages of faith development, the spiritual caregiver can help the person to examine the values that he or she has received from the group in the light now of his or her own life experience.

I find that in the movement from the conventional to the individuative/reflective stages, counseling issues can arise from the guilt of not always following or even sharply disagreeing with the norms of a person's group at the literalizing or conventional stages of faith development. Counselors facilitating a deeper level of spiritual consciousness can enable people to find their own authority and at the same time live with the authority of the group. In more developed later stages of faith, when a person's meaning is more universal and globally focused, scripture and spiritual care could be used in a "search for love and justice through self-surrender" (Ivy, 1987, p. 339). The counselor helps the client find more universal compassion for the self, for others, and the world.

Spiritual Experience Index (Spiritual Maturity)

In essence the developmental approach to spiritual assessment looks toward the spiritual maturity of the person. Genia's (1991, 1997) spiritual experience index assesses spiritual maturity in contrast to spiritual immaturity. In her research, Genia determines that a person needs a "balance" of two qualities for spiritual maturity: spiritual support and spiritual openness. Spiritual support takes place through a commitment to a particular spiritual path in a community context, and spiritual openness takes place through the ability to perceive and integrate spirituality beyond a person's particular community and chosen path.

When a person focuses completely on spiritual support within his or her community, without spiritual openness, he or she becomes "exclusive and rigid" in his or her spirituality. When he or she focuses on spiritual openness without a commitment to a particular community spiritual path, he or she "lacks spiritual rootedness" and the growth that it brings (1997, p. 356). The combination of the two results in spiritual maturity. Genia lists eleven significant criteria for spiritual maturity:

1. Transcendent relationship to something greater than oneself
2. Consistency of lifestyle, including moral behavior with spirit values
3. Commitment without absolute certainty
4. Appreciation of spiritual diversity
5. Absence of egocentricity and magical thinking
6. Equal emphasis on both reason and emotion
7. Mature concern for others
8. Tolerance and human growth strongly encouraged
9. Struggles to understand evil and suffering
10. A felt sense of meaning and purpose
11. Ample room for both traditional beliefs and private interpretations (Genia, 1997, p. 345, criteria reprinted with permission)

The following are some statements from Genia's spiritual experience index, under her two categories of the need for (1) spiritual support, and (2) spiritual openness in order to attain spiritual maturity.

Spiritual Support

1. I often feel strongly related to a power greater than myself.
2. My faith gives my life meaning and purpose.
3. My faith is a way of life.
4. My relationship to God is experienced as unconditional love.
5. My faith helps me confront tragedy and suffering.
6. Sharing my faith with others is important for my spiritual growth. (Genia, 1997, p. 361, list reprinted with permission)

Spiritual Openness

1. Ideas from faiths different from my own may increase my understanding of spiritual truth.
2. I believe that the world is basically good.

3. Learning about different faiths is an important part of my spiritual development.
4. I feel a strong spiritual bond with all of humankind.
5. My spiritual beliefs change as I encounter new ideas and experiences.
6. Persons of different faiths share a common spiritual bond. (Genia, 1997, p. 361, list reprinted with permission)

Reflection Questions: Of the three developmental models of spiritual assessment, which appeals to you and your work? Developmentally, how is your spiritual growth a lifelong journey? At what stage of spiritual growth do you see yourself in the Capps and Ivy models? What do you think of Genia's belief that spiritual maturity comes from both spiritual support and spiritual openness, and not only a person's individual spiritual search?

SEMISTRUCTURED INTERVIEW AND SURVEYS

Elizabeth McSherry (1987b), a medical doctor from the VA medical center in Roxbury, Massachusetts, popularized in chaplaincy work the semistructured interview. This semistructured interview encompassed meeting and interviewing a helpee, asking questions about the person's spirituality/religion with either the helpee filling out a survey or the helper recording the responses on a standardized form. McSherry, from the mid-1980s to the early 1990s, became the spokesperson for the need for chaplains to document their clinical spiritual work. She stressed that if spiritual care workers wanted to maintain professional status, they would have to adopt a clinically reportable method of spiritually interviewing their helpees. She showed them how to do this through an instrument that she developed, the SPA (spiritual profile assessment). McSherry used this instrument in a semistructured interview. The SPA contains three objective instruments: (1) the Westberg-modified Holmes stress inventory with an additional spirituality section, (2) the three-question Kasl epidemiology scale assessing religiosity, and (3) a list of eighteen ultimate values with the helpee ranking the top three values. All three instruments together take ten to fifteen minutes to complete. To begin the process, the spiritual caregiver would introduce himself or herself briefly and say to the helpee something such as, "Our hospital wants to work with you as a whole person, not only your physical well-being but also your spiritual well-being—body, mind, and spirit. Could you please fill out this short questionnaire for us?"

McSherry stated that through the use of a semistructured interview in an initial hospital meeting, the chaplain could expand the patient's self-reflection on his or her health situation to include a spiritual/religious viewpoint. Usually a person's admission to a hospital, even when the illness is not serious, sets in motion a time of questioning about the meaning of his or her life and even future death. A person's concerns about physical health can become an opportunity for spiritual growth. Both the initial inquiry of the chaplain and the completion of the instruments would bring spiritual/religious concerns out into the open for examination and spiritual support. The patient's openness to and drawing upon spiritual energy would significantly increase the possibility of effective healing for that person. Note, however, that the spiritual caregiver, out of respect for each patient, needs to decide when to use assessment instruments such as these in a semistructured interview. Weakness or sickness on the part of the patient may easily prevent their completion. In a semistructured interview, I find an adapted version of three questions from the Kasl's Religious Spiritual Index to be useful (McSherry, 1987c) (see Figure 4.4) depending on one's own setting.

Counselors might use the questions toward developing three or four of their own introductory questions as part of an initial client intake form. A few questions concerning spirituality/religion in the intake form indicate to clients that they can later talk openly and freely of spiritual or religious concerns. If the completed questions indicate that the clients were spiritual or religious and their problems relate to their spirituality/religion, counselors also could more freely examine these concerns. When appropriate, they could use clients' spirituality/religion for change, growth, and support. Adding spirituality/religion questions to the larger psychosocial questionnaires helps clients realize that spirituality and religion are an ordinary part of human development.

Directions: Circle or check the item most descriptive of you in each of the next three questions.

1. How often did you participate in religious services or formal spiritual activities during the year?

    1. Never   4. Weekly

    2. Major holidays only   5. More than once a week

    3. Occasionally

2. Aside from how often you participate in religious services or formal spiritual activities, do you consider yourself to be:

    1. Very religious/spiritual   3. Only slightly religious/spiritual

    2. Fairly religious/spiritual   4. Not at all religious/spiritual

3. How much is religion/spirituality a source of strength and comfort to you?

    1. Not very much   3. Quite a bit

    2. Somewhat   4. A great deal

FIGURE 4.4. Religious/Spiritual Index (*Source:* Adapted from McSherry, 1987c, p. 5.)

DEVELOPING YOUR OWN SURVEY QUESTIONS

In addition to formal spiritual assessment instruments and questions from other surveys, you may wish to develop your own questions for your work or center. To give you some ideas, some examples from some typical surveys follow. These are some spiritual/religious questions used as part of a questionnaire for bereavement support services.

Circle the letter that best fits your opinion (A = agree; U = undecided; D = disagree).

1. My life has meaning and purpose.	A	U	D
2. I feel hopeful about the future.	A	U	D
3. Religious and/or spiritual issues are important to me.	A	U	D
4. I believe in a Higher Power.	A	U	D
5. I receive strength and support from a Higher Power.	A	U	D

6. I participate in a spiritual and/or faith   A   U   D
   community.
7. My spirituality/faith sustains me in dif-   A   U   D
   ficult times.
8. I find comfort in certain spiritual/reli-   A   U   D
   gious rituals.

Following are some typical questions that might be found on a spiritual survey used in a counseling center:

1. What values or morals were important to your family of origin?
   _____
2. Describe your religious training as a child: _____
3. What is your present religion? _____
4. Are you currently active in church, a religious group, or a spiritual way of life?
   ___ Yes. Describe: _____
   ___ No. Do you want to become active? _____
5. What do you presently believe God or a Higher Power is?___
   _____
6. Do you have any negative feelings toward God, a Higher Power, or religion? _____
7. What do you see as your purpose in life? _____

The following is a brief survey used with substance abuse:

1. Growing up, what was your experience with religion or spirituality? _____
2. When drugs or alcohol entered your life how did that affect your relationship with your Higher Power or God? _____
   _____
3. How do you feel today about God or religion? _____
   _____
4. What are your hopes for the future and does a Higher Power play a role in their fulfillment? _____

For some effective survey questions where spirituality/religion enters closely into psychological and counseling issues, see Figure 4.5.

1. Are religious or spiritual issues important in your life?
   ___ Yes ___ No ___ Somewhat
2. Do you wish to discuss them in counseling, when relevant?
   ___ Yes ___ No
   If not, you do not need to answer the remaining questions about religion and spirituality.
3. Do you believe in God or a Supreme Being? ___Yes ___ No
   Please elaborate if you wish _____
   _____
   _____

4. Do you believe you can experience spiritual guidance? ___ Yes ___ No
   If so, how often have you had such experiences:
   ___ Often ___ Occasionally ___ Rarely ___ Never
5. What is your current religious affiliation (if any)?_____

6. Are you committed to it and actively involved? ___ Yes ___ Somewhat ___ No
7. What was your childhood religious affiliation (if any)? _____

8. How important was religion or spiritual beliefs to you as a child and adolescent?
   ___Important ___ Somewhat important ___ Unimportant
   Please elaborate if you wish _____

9. Are you aware of any religious or spiritual resources in your life that could be used to
   help you overcome your problems? ___ Yes ___ No
   If yes, what are they? _____

10. Do you believe that religious or spiritual influences have hurt you or contributed to some
    of your problems? ___ Yes ___ No
    If yes, can you briefly explain how? _____

11. Would you like your counselor to consult with your religious leader if it appears this could
    be helpful to you? ___ Yes ___ No ___ Maybe
    If yes, a permission and confidentiality form will be provided for you to sign.
12. Are you willing to consider trying religious or spiritual suggestions from your counselor if it
    appears that they could be helpful to you? ___ Yes ___ No

FIGURE 4.5. Richards and Bergin's Religious/Spiritual Client Intake Assessment Questions (*Source:* P. Scott Richards and Allen E. Bergin, 1997. *A Spiritual Strategy for Counseling and Psychotherapy,* p. 193. Copyright ©1997 by the American Psychological Association. Reprinted with permission.)

GUIDELINES FOR THE DEVELOPMENT OF SPIRITUAL ASSESSMENT SURVEYS

Now that you have some ideas of possible questions for your own spiritual assessment survey form, let us now consider some guidelines or parameters for developing such a survey form to be used either at intake or periodically during a longer course of counseling. Obviously the language used should be understandable by those completing the assessment form. Also, common sense tells us that the type of form, the kinds of information sought, and the questions asked would depend on your center and the helpees that it serves. As we can see from the previous examples, a survey form for a center working primarily with substance abuse clients has a slightly different focus than a more general intake form. The former assumes that the helpee is familiar with the terminology of Alcoholics Anonymous, and the latter survey focuses on the possible integration of spirituality/religion into a traditional counseling situation. Moreover, with a particular form or survey a helper needs to determine whether the helpee or the helper will fill out the form. In a brief semistructured interview the helper most probably would ask some basic questions and complete the form. If further information is desired, the helper could leave a survey to be filled out later by the helpee. In some settings, such as hospital chaplaincy, the chaplain frequently fills out two forms after talking with the helpee, one for his or her own and/or the department's reference, plus a second form may be completed in the hospital chart itself, which is kept at the nurses' station.

The following is an example of such a two-step format of spiritual assessment. The first step or form is for the caregiver's own use (Figure 4.6), and the second step or form documentation is for the broader staff (Figure 4.7).

---

1) Kind of Contact _____

2) Focus of Helping _____

3) Concerns or Problems Raised _____

4) Service Provided _____

5) Result _____

    The Helpee's Spiritual Needs:
        Lack of Meaning ⟶ Richness of Meaning
        Unable to Receive Love/Care ⟶ Able to Receive Love/Care
        Unable to Give Love/Care ⟶ Able to Give Love/Care
        Cannot Forgive Self ⟶ Can Forgive Self
        Cannot Forgive Others ⟶ Can Forgive Others
        In Hopelessness ⟶ In Hope

FIGURE 4.6. Spiritual Assessment Form for the Caregiver's Use (*Source:* Adapted from Arnold, 1996, p. 13.)

Spiritual Assessment and Care

Helpee's name_____

Present Emotional Status

(Check feelings, signs, and/or symptoms exhibited by the helpee which may be indicative of spiritual needs.)

[ ] Fear of_____	[ ] Loneliness	[ ] Manipulative
[ ] Acceptance	[ ] Bitterness	[ ] Talks continually
[ ] Guilt	[ ] Crying	[ ] Despair
[ ] Grief/loss	[ ] Loss of control	[ ] Appears to sleep continually
[ ] Anger	[ ] Control issues	[ ] Self-destructive behavior
[ ] Denial	[ ] Cynicism	[ ] Inappropriate behavior
[ ] Low self-esteem	[ ] Withdrawal	
[ ] Signs of anxiety	[ ] Other:_____	

Relationship to Spiritual Needs

(Meaning, Deeper Connections of Care and Love, Forgiveness, Hope)

_____
_____
_____

Religious/Faith Background

Denomination: _____ Church: _____

Patient: [ ] Important [ ] Noncommittal [ ] Unimportant [ ] Unknown
Family: [ ] Important [ ] Noncommittal [ ] Unimportant [ ] Unknown

Sacraments or Religious Rituals requested: [ ] Yes [ ] No [ ] N/A

Comments: _____
_____

Current Support Systems

___Church ___Family ___Friends ___Institutional Care ___Agency
___Other: _____

Comments: _____

Helper's Signature: _____ Date: _____

FIGURE 4.7. Spiritual Assessment Form for Staff Documentation (*Source:* Adapted from *Quality Assurance and Pastoral Care,* the Catholic Health Association, 1990, pp. 56-57. Copyright ©1990 by the Catholic Health Association. Adapted with permission.)

Regardless of the type of form developed, certain guidelines are called for. The questions need to be clear, concise, and "salient" (Farran et al., 1989, p. 189), that is, related to life situations and people. The form needs to be comprehensive or "multidimensional"

(Fitchett, 1993, p. 40). For instance, an ideal form would examine spiritual assessment from a religious as well as a nonreligious belief system (Hay, 1989). Both would be acceptable and enhanced. Also, there needs to be a strong assumption in the survey questions that a person's spirituality is integrated into the whole person, and that spirituality is a developmental process. The focus is not just substantive, (What do you believe?), but more functional (How do you live your spirituality?). Particularly with regard to clarity, what do the initiators of the form see as spirituality and spiritual needs? Does the form use a language of spirituality that makes a distinction between psychological needs and spiritual needs or are they both viewed as the same? In this regard, Hay (1989), from a hospice point of view, speaks of how so often spiritual assessment forms assess spiritual needs only in psychological language.

I have attempted in this book to develop a clinical language of spirituality to assess specific spiritual needs. Does your developed form use such a language of spirituality? True, spiritual needs may not be as self-evident as psychosocial needs. Spiritual needs appear clearly in only the most painful situations, when psychological and social resources fail. Nonetheless, we need to continue to develop such a language of spirituality.

When considering the outlay of the survey form itself, is its length appropriate? How much effort and time can be expected of the helpee or the helper? If the helper is completing the form for helpees, will the helper need training to satisfactorily complete it? Finally, how will the information obtained from the form be interpreted? Will the helper use categories for the person such as spiritual health, spiritual well-being, and spiritual distress? Farran et al. (1989) speak of the individual "functioning at a maintenance level, an expanded [very healthy] level or an altered [unbalanced] level" (p. 193). Will there be a section for goals and possible interventions with potential outcomes?

In sum, how complete will the survey be and still remain manageable and practical? Of course, no form is perfect. It is best to begin the process and learn from it. If you wait until the form is perfect, very little will be accomplished. We have already waited too long to develop a clinical method to assess our helpees' spiritual needs and strengths in order to offer them more effective spiritual care and healing.

Chapter 5

Basic Aptitudes and Skills
of Spiritual Care

Spiritual care is assisting an individual with her or his spiritual needs and development. It is bringing an awareness and connectedness with a person's spirit into one's life concerns. Who is competent to undertake spiritual care? What skills and aptitudes do capable spiritual care practitioners need? As professional caregivers we have always focused on developing relationship and communication skills to work with peoples' psyches and emotions. Now, we need to tap the spiritual dimension of this process. We have viewed spirituality as the integrative principle of a whole person. Similarly, our task with regard to spiritual care skills is not so much a need to add new techniques of spirituality to our repertoire as to value spirit and integrate spirituality into our present skill level. We do this when we focus on spiritual growth and development as part of normal human growth and development. We care for the whole person, body, mind, and emotions within the context of the spiritual dimension. In essence, our challenge in this chapter is to learn how to integrate spirituality within whole-person care. We are not so much externally applying specific skills to a person but facilitating spiritual growth within him or her.

Spiritual care is not primarily learning a new technology of skills and techniques. Rather, it is a way of being. It is an intentional attitude that respects and cherishes a person as a spirited organism with spiritual needs. Spiritual care is a lived philosophy. Spiritual caregivers believe that a person marvelously heals and grows spiritually from within. The spiritual care competencies of the spiritual caregiver primarily come from the attitudes and values of the spiritual caregiver. Helpers' mind-sets and intentions create the possibility and the kind of spiritual care. For example, how we view human nature or a person will determine our spiritual care no matter what skills of helping we employ. If we view a person as rational, positive, and capable of an active role in personal change, we will do spiritual care differently than if we view him or her as filled with weakness, irrationality, and in need of much external help to bring about change. The first spiritual caregiver, believing in the person's internal spirit, will trust the person to grow spiritually from within; and the second will be more concerned with external behavior techniques to bring about change.

In sum, the competent spiritual caregiver sees the person as a subject with whom to relate rather than an object to be changed. Indeed research strongly shows that "more effective counselors [helpers] tend to see people as able, dependable, friendly, and worthy [subjects in themselves]. Less effective counselors [helpers] have serious doubts about such human qualities in their clients" (Combs, 1989, p. 76). More than the skills, the spiritual care practitioner's attitudes and belief system about a person determine the process of spiritual care.

ABILITY TO DEVELOP A CARING AND HEALING HELPING RELATIONSHIP

This book has already taught many core competencies in spiritual care. We have identified and become more observant of spirituality in the human person, learned how to assess spiritual needs, and employed instruments of spiritual assessment. However, in doing spiritual care, none of these skills accomplishes spiritual growth in the helpee unless the spiritual caregiver first successfully establishes a helping relationship with the helpee. If there is no connection, little or no spiritual care, much less internal healing, can take place. The word that we use is "care." If a person really cares for another, he or she is involved in some type of a relationship with the person. Care means that a person shows concern for someone, knows, and is connected to the person in some way. Spiritual care is an interactional process where relationship is its key.

Research on "relationship-centered care" (Pew-Fetzer Task Force, 1994) is under way in the health care professions. Medical professionals in particular realize that medical technology alone is not the key to quality care. A person is not just a sick body part treated with technology. When a person is respected and treated as a whole, his or her relationship with the health care provider can be the most important and the most curative aspect of health care. A disease may be alleviated with technology, but true whole-person health care happens in relationship-centered care.

Likewise, relationship-centered care is the foundation and integrative core of effective spiritual care. Only out of relationship-centered care can spiritual care providers effectively use the models of spiritual needs that we have been discussing. Moreover, in this regard the first and primary focus of spiritual care is on the person rather than the task at hand. With all our attention on identifying spiritual needs and completing a spiritual assessment, we could mistakenly focus only on the task and bypass the person. Spiritual care is person-centered rather than task-centered. Only out of the focus on and communication with the person come the work and the tasks of spiritual care. We saw earlier that healing and spiritual growth happens when a person experiences deeper connection, finds enriched meaning, and receives and gives love. Is this not what a caring and healing helping relationship accomplishes? Spiritual care is not something that one person does for another. It happens within the helpee in the interaction between the spiritual caregiver and helpee. Spiritual care is a caring and healing relationship, and interaction of the spiritual care practitioner with the helper assisting the person in his or her spiritual needs and development toward spiritual well-being. To establish a caring and healing helping relationship, to richly appreciate its effectiveness, and to fervently affirm its spiritual capacity, are the most important skills of the spiritual care practitioner.

Counseling psychology has termed a caring and healing relationship a "helping relationship" (Rogers, 1958). This term is not used loosely. Counselors understand it as a relationship with specific describable characteristics. For example, in our spiritual care work, a helping relationship is different from and more than a social-friendly relationship. It is different from only caring camaraderie, different even from friendship. A helping relationship is one wherein the helper focuses on the helpee's growth rather than a conversation between friends who equally exchange information and ideas. In friendship there is a mutual concern for each other, and each helps the other. However, in a helping relationship, the helper is not outwardly helped by the helpee; nor are they establishing a friendship. Rather, the helper establishes a more expert helping relationship, looking toward the growth of the helpee. In spiritual care the helper looks toward the person's spiritual needs and well-being. Indeed in a spiritually focused helping relationship, the helper is more of a listener to the helpee's needs and concerns.

It is sometimes said that in a helping relationship, whoever characteristically does the most talking is the person who is getting the help. The helper's listening facilitates the helpee, exploring concerns while talking and reflecting on what is said. It is a helpee-centered approach to helping. As a student recently said to me, "I want to come to talk with you so that I can figure out what is happening with me." As the helper in a helping relationship I listen, responding to the person and helping clarify his or her concerns. A helping relationship naturally leads to a focus on the person and the whole-person care that is at the core of spiritual care. It shows true care on the part of the helper and frequently leads to deeper connection and meaning or spiritual growth on the part of the helpee.

The following list notes the differing conversational focuses between a helping relationship and a social-friendly relationship.

Helping Relationship	Social-Friendly Relationship
1. Respecting the person (How are they hurting?)	External subjects—weather, world events, local events
2. Helping the person share self in here and now	Sharing stories, experiences, mutual trading
3. Comfort through facing pain and hurt	Comfort through avoiding hurt
4. Accepting tension areas in people's lives	Maintaining a congenial atmosphere
5. Being concrete and specific (what a helpee does, thinks, feels)	Speaking in generalities (what people do and say)
6. Being understanding, empathetic	Being pleasant, positive, or sympathetic
7. Helping helpees share personal experiences	Being helpful by entertaining

In a helping relationship our energies as spiritual caregivers center on the other person sharing self, his or her concerns, and what the person is presently thinking and feeling. The helping relationship reaches down to a depth of feeling and person.

Jesus exhibited strong helping relationships when He assisted the two disciples on the road to Emmaus who were grieving his crucifixion and death. To help them comprehend the pain of their loss, Jesus first completely listened to their story and felt with them their fears and loss. He walked and waited with them. He did not simply exchange information with them or try to console them and help them feel more positive. Rather, he helped them first explore what had happened and what they thought and felt about it. In a true helping relationship, He focused on their anxieties and compassionately listened to their needs. Only out of their story and pain did He then facilitate their finding deeper meaning, spiritual growth, and healing. This indeed is the process of spiritual care in a helping relationship. From a listening relationship with a spiritual caregiver, the helpee comes to a deeper connection and an expanded meaning of life. As Jesus was walking with the disciples and talking or listening to them in a helping relationship, they became aware of an intense spiritual truth and reason for living with hope and joy in their lives. They said, "It is the Lord," as they recognized Him in the breaking of the bread.

In sum, Jesus looks to the spiritual care of others through first relating to them as persons in a helping relationship, not just a social relationship. He understands, listens, and feels with people. He does not guide and advise them or cover over their pain, but brings comfort to others through acknowledging and helping them face their pain. From feeling this pain with the other, He heals the pain and brings spiritual meaning. Other examples of Jesus' way of helping include His conversations with the woman caught in adultery or the woman at the well. We see and name Jesus here as a great teacher, but He teaches most of all through modeling for us compassionate care through a strong helping relationship. Such a relationship heals and brings spiritual growth.

Reflection Questions: The skill of the helping relationship seems so obvious. However, do you as a caregiver, especially in noncrisis situations, focus first on developing a helping relationship with the helpee? Or do you focus on what the helpee needs to do or what you can do for the helpee? Do you understand the difference between a friendship and a helping relationship? How do you think people grow and change? What has enabled you in the past to grow and change: advice, warning, listening, preaching, etc.?

The Three Characteristics of a Skillful Helping Relationship

How can we as spiritual practitioners develop the kind of helping relationship that leads to meaning and spiritual healing in others? How can we create a climate for spiritual growth and change? Counselors and psychologists, through their practice of helping countless people over the past several decades, have discovered a series of three specific steps or attitudes on the part of the caregiver (Rogers, 1958) that lead to an effective helping relationship and change on the part of the helpee. These steps are

1. unconditional positive regard and acceptance of the other person,
2. empathy with the person, and
3. genuineness on the part of the caregiver.

They almost appear too simple to be effective. However, they are harder to accomplish in a practical way than you might think. They are important for us as spiritual care practitioners because their implementation positively influences the establishment and development of quality spiritual care.

Unconditional Positive Regard

The spiritual caregiver shows unconditional positive regard and acceptance of the person when he or she reaches out to accept the person as he or she is. This means respecting, prizing, even celebrating the person in front of you in an unpossessive and confirming way. Mother Teresa, in her care for the dying, stated that she aimed not so much to help the person but rather to prize the person as Christ. All religious traditions speak of a person as made in the image and likeness of God. Do we see that, hear that, and feel the very image of God in helpees when we work with them, no matter who they are or what they have done? God's reflection, the reflection of love, is found in some way in each helpee. Likewise, in regard to Spirit, do we see the Spirit within the person and trust its resources to bring about change from within? Can we wait, trusting our own intuition, and at the same time draw upon the wisdom of the Spirit for guidance?

Carl Rogers (1961), speaking of unconditional positive regard and acceptance, says, "By acceptance I mean a warm regard for him [one] as a person of unconditional self worth—of value no matter what [the] condition, behavior, or feelings" (p. 34). A spiritual term for unconditional positive regard and acceptance would certainly be love in the sense of the Greek *agape.* It is freely accepting and loving the other for the sake of the other. Recently, I asked several spiritual directors what they saw as the key qualities of a good spiritual director. Not knowing how the others had responded, each director named the ability to accept the directee as he or she is as the most important quality of an effective spiritual director. They agreed with Rogers that our attitudes and feelings are the most important elements in helping. On a continuum of some acceptance to much acceptance, where do you fall with your helpees with respect to positive regard and positive acceptance, especially those who are different from you? Remember that positive regard and acceptance of others is always a process. It is never complete. The spiritual caregiver keeps attempting to live it.

A Continuum of Acceptance

Some acceptance   →   Much acceptance
and positive regard   and positive regard

Communicating unconditional positive regard and acceptance does not mean that the spiritual caregiver avoids challenging and compassionately confronting the helpee in her or his life's discrepancies and destructive behaviors (Clinebell, 1984). Helpee guilt is not always uncalled for, neurotic, or toxic. The helpee may indeed have played a negative role in a particular situation. The resultant guilt is healthy and appropriate and can be faced and healed. Compassionate confrontation on the helper's part enables the helpee to think about concerns in new and creative ways and facilitates change and growth. This type of helping relationship accomplishes healing through a combination of deep-accepting listening of the person together with a challenging call to a healthier ethical life.

For example, a helpee speaks of an inability to find a committed relationship, but at the same time tells a story of using people sexually. The spiritual caregiver explains the meaning of a healthy committed relationship and points out the usual unhappy consequences of this practice. He or she creatively confronts the helpee, pointing out the inconsistency of his or her behavior. The helper inquires of the helpee how he or she might develop more fulfilling relationships. Regardless of helpee guilt, throughout the discussion, the helper continually cherishes, cares for, and prizes the person in a helping relationship. God loves us as we are and yet challenges us and looks to the spiritual wholeness we might achieve.

Reflection Questions: With regard to your helpees, notice your non-verbal clues, especially your eye contact, body position, and sound of your voice. How focused are they on the helpee? These will tell you much about your level of regard for the other. If you were a helpee, what signs of acceptance would you look for from a spiritual care-giver? Finally, are there any groups of people that you have difficulty accepting? Honestly face this. If you do not grow in accepting them, think about referring the spiritual care of these people to another.

Empathy

The spiritual caregiver feels and expresses empathy with the person. Helpers make a distinction between sympathy and empathy. Sympathy means that a person is sorry for someone else because of his or her condition. Empathy, on the other hand, means truly "feeling with" the person and his or her condition. Each helpee has his or her own meaning and feelings about his or her situation. A truly empathetic helper understands a person from the inside. For example, if a person is worried whether he or she has cancer, the spiritual caregiver can feel sorrow or sympathy for the person, or he or she can really feel the fear of cancer with and inside the person. In other words, to be empathetic is to enter the helpee's world or his or her internal frame of reference. It is an attempt to help and care through seeing and feeling a person's world as he or she sees and feels it. This is much more effective than pity or sympathy for the person.

Empathy is a spiritual process, since it is lived compassion for helpees. Through listening with empathy we feel and suffer with them. We roll into the background our own selves and needs, deny ourselves, and empty ourselves and leave space for the story and feelings of the helpee. We practice what spiritually is sometimes termed "poverty of spirit." This empathy, feeling with the helpee, naturally creates an open space for the Spirit, God, to more fully come into the helping concern and relationship. The helpee looks inward and draws strength there. God speaks there in ways that we could not have imagined. Too often we are unwilling to listen long enough to our helpees. We think that the helpee does not know enough. We need to grow in trust of the Spirit working within the helpee. Real change happens when people are really listened to. Have you ever been fully listened to—felt that someone really understood you and felt your pain with you? Empathy is a process of spirituality because it is a process of helpee and helper transcending themselves by listening, seeking, and finding deeper meaning. The end result is that both are more present to each other and to God in a deeper spiritual connection. Both more fully experience spiritual well-being.

I find that spiritual caregivers sometimes simplistically assume that they are empathetic because they themselves know and feel in their hearts how much they really care for people. However, even though they really care for people, their empathy must be outwardly shown. The helpee needs to know, experience, and see the caregiver's empathy. He or she does this by listening well.

This is only the first step, however. The second important step is to let the helpee know in an external way that you really hear him or her. This can be accomplished with your words and nonverbal body language. For example, if someone tells the caregiver that she or he is fearful that she or he has cancer, the caregiver needs to let the person know that she or he hears the fear. One way that this second step is successfully accomplished is to respond to the helpee's original statement with a paraphrase of the helpee's statement in the helper's own words. The spiritual caregiver may respond with words such as, "So you are nervous and scared that you have cancer." The ineffective and nonempathetic helper might respond with, "Try to think positive until you know the results," or even cover over the helpee's fear of cancer by saying, "I'll pray for you."

Empathy then needs not only to be felt inside the helper but also needs to be conveyed in an outward way through the helper's words and body language. When this is done effectively, a third completing step usually takes place with the helpee responding to the helper that he or she has been heard. The helpee acknowledges this with some word or phrase such as simply "Yes" or "That's correct." With the woman with cancer, she might respond, saying: "Yes, I am afraid of dying."

To conclude, empathy means truly listening to and feeling with the person rather than just hearing the story. If I only hear the story, I know what the person is saying. However, if I truly listen, I focus on the person who is speaking. There is a wide gap between hearing and listening. Real empathy with true listening is hard work.

Genuineness

The spiritual caregiver is genuine as a person in the caring relationship. He or she must be real and authentic. The caregiver cannot just play the role of the caregiver. This brings too much distance between the caregiver and the helpee. Although people do come to us because of our roles as caregivers, they also need to see and experience us as sincere human persons in our roles. However, the caregiver cannot be so real and so genuine that he or she comes across as an ordinary Joe and hence does not appear competent in the role of a spiritual caregiver. Nor can you just play the role. When this happens, the helper frequently comes across as aloof, insincere, and artificial. For example, a counselor or a chaplain cannot figuratively wear a mask carrying out the role of a counselor or chaplain. Rather, she or he needs to be a real person in the role of counselor or chaplain.

We especially show genuineness as spiritual caregivers when we are congruent—that is, when we are honestly in touch with our own feelings, spirit, and spirituality. A certain depth of presence is then communicated to the helpee. The Spirit comes alive. We communicate to the helpee that we are genuinely interested in his or her spiritual care and growth.

Reflection Questions: Can you develop a helping relationship? Can you listen and wait with helpees in their struggles and pain? Or do you cover over their pain? Once the pain is felt, can you help them identify and draw on their positive assets to work with their concerns? How do you view yourself in a helping relationship: an advisor giving information, a detective solving the problem, a doctor fixing the problem, or a facilitator enabling the other to heal? Is one more prominent than the other? Which do you see as most effective?

ABILITY TO BRING SPIRITUAL AWARENESS INTO THE HELPING RELATIONSHIP

The effective spiritual caregiver has the ability to expand and integrate the helping relationship through a more explicit spiritual connection. He or she needs to know how to nurture the spiritual self. Spiritual awareness is brought to helpees' concerns and problems through relating them to deeper connections and meaning. When the helper touches the meaning of a helpee's life, he or she touches that helpee's spirituality. When the helpee searches for deeper meaning of his or her situation, he or she discovers his or her spirituality. To accomplish the end of reaching a deeper spiritual connection, the helper may ask such open-ended questions as, "What gives you comfort?" or "Where do you go when you are hurt?"

The following model depicts this progression from a helping-psychological focus expanded to a spiritual care focus.

A Helping-Psychological Focus	**A Spiritual Care Focus**
1. Helping helpees share their problems/concerns in the here and now	Helping helpees share their problems within the context of their deepest meaning and connections
2. Working with tension areas in helpees' lives	Exploring the relationship between a person's spirituality/religion and tension areas
3. Enabling helpees to find ways to solve their problems	Enabling helpees to find hope in life and acceptance of problems when unsolvable
4. Being empathetic, understanding	Relating to the helpee from the perspective of universal love, a child of God
5. Significant relationships of the person	The helpee's relationship to the universe, to a Higher Power, to God

6. Comfort through facing pain and hurt	Comfort through exploring wider connections in and beyond the person's own pain and hurt
7. Focus on human adjustment	Focus on spiritual/religious experience (high-level wellness)

Acknowledging spirituality and infusing spiritual care into a helping relationship is simply going one step further in the professional helping relationship. Spiritual care is taking the helpee's present issues and concerns and helping her or him develop a deeper spiritual or meaning perspective around these issues and concerns. It is not an external process or even adding another layer to the helping relationship. Rather, it is acknowledging and reaching for the deepest connections in a person's human growth and development, and his or her spirit and spirituality. This spiritual awareness brings a person spiritual empowerment. In spirituality, a person develops a larger sense of control in his or her life, and out of this expanded sense of control comes inner spiritual healing.

For example, a client presents with an issue of tremendous stress in her or his life. In a helping relationship, the counselor would help the client look at the physical and emotional demands of life leading up to the stress. The client would look at the pressure and tensions of her or his life and decide what to do with her or his problems and self. Moving to a spiritual focus in the helping relationship, the counselor would facilitate the client looking at the meaning of stress in relationship to the client's larger connections beyond ego deep within the self. Where does the client find her or his core strength and hope? The stressful client might alleviate stress through connecting into a wider spiritual path of meditation or through quiet time in religious prayer. Her or his stress might be relieved through a spirited walk in nature, which brings expanded connections to the human person.

In sum, a helping relationship is the foundation of all spiritual care. An effective helper shows a true care of a person in that he or she accepts the helpee unconditionally, truly empathizes with his or her concerns, and facilitates the helper and helpee's authentic selves. As a result, deeper meaning, closer connections, and healing and hope in life grow. A helping relationship becomes one of spiritual care as the helpee's spirituality and spiritual needs for meaning, deep connection, and hope are acknowledged in the helping relationship. This spiritual awareness can bring spiritual well-being. Psychological health is integrated with spiritual care, and this fulfillment of spiritual needs leads not only to psychological health but also to spiritual wellness.

KNOWLEDGE AND ACCEPTANCE OF YOUR IDENTITY AS A SPIRITUAL CAREGIVER

Helping professionals may hesitate to accept the identity of spiritual caregiver. They may think that this identity is for religious professionals, not for secular helpers. However, as discussed earlier, spirituality is part of every person's psyche whether or not his or her spirituality is religious. Moreover, as caregivers, even when we do attempt to integrate a client's spirituality into our helping practice, we may frequently see ourselves as ineffective instruments of spiritual care. This is not unusual. Being human, our spiritual care is never perfect and always open to improvement and growth. Perfect spiritual care and the perfect spiritual caregiver are both illusions.

Spiritual caregiving is not for the helper who has a need to do it perfectly (Burns, 1980). As Burns points out, the caregiver who does an ordinary job is usually more effective than the perfectionist. When we concentrate on doing perfect spiritual care, we focus more on ourselves than on the helpee, and lose the core human relationship focus of caring. Sometimes as spiritual caregivers we have almost a messiah complex. We need to do it perfectly and be the saviors. In helping others, we reflect back that we did not do all that we could have and all that others expected us to do. There is that obsessive feeling of "I never listened enough. I did not reach out enough." In striving for our own excellence, we can even lose the joy of our work. We burn out, feel guilty, and suffer discouragement and even depression. A more effective way is to do an ordinary, good-enough job by rolling back our focus on self. This allows space for the Spirit to enter more easily into our relationship with the helpee. God uses us, and we become effective instruments of the Spirit. Knowing both our inadequacies and competencies, we need to accept our identities as spiritual caregivers.

People frequently do not see themselves as possessing a particular quality or ability unless they live it almost 100 percent of the time.

People struggle to fully accept the good in themselves. If you ask someone whether he or she is a caring person, you might be surprised at the response. He or she might reflect that he or she was most unkind last week to a particular person; therefore he or she is not really a caring person. Yet 90 percent of the time he or she is kind and cares. Why is it that we need to have a characteristic almost 100 percent of the time to accept ourselves as possessing it? If we show anger even 15 percent of the time, we consider ourselves angry people. For whatever reason, we often judge ourselves based on our weaknesses and inadequacies rather than our strengths and good qualities.

For example, many people would accept their identities as writers only after they have published. They need to be expert at it before they can call themselves writers. However, Julia Cameron (1998), in *The Right to Write*, states that a person needs to accept self as a writer simply because he or she simply begins to write regardless of publication. Writing makes a person a writer. Can you accept at least a beginning identity as a spiritual caregiver simply because you are already doing spiritual care?

In my early days of chaplaincy training, I remember how the supervisor struggled with the new interns to accept our identities as chaplains. The supervisor wanted to know how we introduced ourselves to patients. Students would answer with statements such as, "Hello, I am Ms. so and so. I am studying to be a chaplain," or "Hello, I am a student intern in chaplaincy. I hope to be a chaplain someday." We had a difficult time accepting identity as chaplains. We thought that this would happen only when we had successfully completed our training. The supervisor encouraged us—I should say argued with us—to state, "Hello, I am Chaplain so and so."

In the first verse of his letter to the Ephesians, St. Paul calls the people in the Church "saints." He recognizes their identities as such even though at times he certainly experienced them also as sinners or less than saints.

The question to reflect on is, do we, even as beginners in spiritual care, accept our calling and identity as spiritual caregivers? As the Apostle Paul points out, the Spirit already lives within us. Do not others feel this spirit and touch the spirit in themselves in our care of them even as novice spiritual caregivers? Goldsmith (1986), reflecting on how God acts in our lives, states that "only in the degree that he [one] acknowledges fulfillment can he [one] achieve fulfillment" (p. 86).

This is an inspiring statement. A person needs to accept the reality that God, from the beginning, works through him or her as a spiritual caregiver. In this way, he or she will continue to grow and find competency and fulfillment as a spiritual caregiver. The reign of God lies within. God is bringing fulfillment through us. In order to do competent spiritual care, we need to bring to consciousness, to know, and to identify that God cares for others through us.

Reflection Questions: How might you view your role as a spiritual caregiver whether you are a beginner or a professional? What would enable you to accept yourself in this role? Can you name a time when you felt ineffective and a time when you felt effective integrating spirituality into your helping? How has God/Spirit used you in both situations? Can you accept your identity as a spiritual caregiver, and at the same time have the courage of imperfection? Can you do a good-enough job and allow God to work through you? How are you growing further in your role and identity as a spiritual caregiver?

Discovering Your Image As a Spiritual Caregiver

As part of this process of accepting your identity as a spiritual caregiver, discovering a spiritual or religious image for yourself as a spiritual caregiver can give you increased energy and a stronger identity. Images strengthen our inner vision. They develop our spiritual consciousness and give meaning to our care. From this consciousness and meaning come a stronger identity and healing abilities. Carl Jung (cited in Dittes, 1990) states that one of the primary growth tasks of mid-age is to discover an "archetype" from which to draw energy to live by. This archetypal energy (image) might be that of the wise woman, a savior, father, mother, companion, etc. Indeed, a psychic, spiritual, or religious image can call us to our life's destiny. Important life events and episodes leave behind for us images to use as models for our work in spiritual care. One woman speaks of how she had taken care of her mother-in-law when she was aging. Now in her pastoral care work with the elderly, she identifies with Ruth from the Hebrew Scriptures. Another woman views herself in spiritual care as a midwife present to others through establishing a caring environment to bring new life. Her image as a spiritual caregiver provides her with daily reminders of God's great love and continued providence.

Such strong feminist images are important today for the many women doing pastoral care and counseling. A man identifies with the story of the prodigal son, however. He sees himself as having strayed and returned to his Father God. Now he sees his pastoral care work helping others return to the same path. Another man who lived as a child with an unpredictable, violent, and abusive father now sees himself as a "wounded celebrator." As an adult, out of the wounded child came forth the natural child. This wound now enables him to experience suffering with others. It prevents him from minimizing their pain. His wound also allows him to experience the depth of life with others and makes him more fully alive.

These and other images enable us to do spiritual care out of our hearts as well as our heads. The head usually calls for achievement and perfection, the heart for care for the other. An image can give you a heart-focused model of spiritual care. For example, from Christian (Campbell, 1981) or other spiritual/religious images, can you see yourself as a wounded healer or wounded celebrator who through your past healed wounds can now reach out in compassion to others? Can you see yourself as the good shepherd who gives his or her life for the sheep? Can you image yourself as a wise fool who in simplicity calls and challenges the other to spiritual growth, well-being, and community?

Of course, we do not want to develop a messiah complex (May, 1989), completely identifying with a chosen image. That might be harmful. However, spiritual images and metaphorical stories (Williams and Williams, 1992) model for us strong roles in spiritual care. Maybe your model is as simple as a person of wisdom or a gardener. It may be a bicycle built for two with God or Spirit riding with you on your journey of spiritual care for others. A recent meeting of 105 priests on "Renewing Priestly Identity" (Traupman, 2000) produced 236 images, such as: bridge builder, juggler, another Christ, disciple, door opener, healer, friend, midwife, patient fisherman, orchestra conductor, and potter or molder. Images indeed give us meaning and psychological and spiritual strength in and for our caregiving journeys.

Experiential Exercise: Spiritual/Religious Lifeline

On a blank sheet of paper, draw a line to represent your life span. Divide your life into periods of time, such as every ten or fifteen years. Reflect on your life as related to spiritual and/or religious experiences, and write down times and situations you feel were important. Reflect on people who influenced your spiritual identity. Do these experiences or people present to you an image of spiritual care that you could use for yourself?

Developing a Prayer Identity As a Spiritual Caregiver

As we care for our own spirits in prayer, we grow in our roles and identities as spiritual caregivers. In such spiritual practices as self-reflection, in quiet time, in meditation, we experience our spirits in the Spirit of God. We raise our levels of spiritual consciousness and realize that God is active in our lives and uses us. We develop confidence to share what we have been given. Our inward-prayer journey freely leads to outward care for others. Spiritual care is not just the task, it is who we are as spiritual persons. Rather than simply making spirituality a task to be integrated into our professional care, we can experience this care for ourselves in prayer. In many ways, spirituality is our capacity for contemplative reflection.

The methods of prayer are many: reflection, meditation, quiet time, listening, music, formal prayers, sacred scripture, liturgies, praise, thanksgiving, centering, etc. Bonhoeffer (1985), in his book *Spiritual Care,* encourages spiritual caregivers in their quiet prayer to bring to mind those for whom they care. He encourages the use of intercessory prayer for helpees. Prayer for them will enable us to listen to them more closely when we meet again. In this way, others will be able to sense that we live in the Spirit as we assist them on their journeys of spiritual healing and wholeness.

We need to balance the practice of spiritual care with placing ourselves in prayer. It is always more tempting to do good rather than to stop and be in the Spirit. Spiritual care for others is done in the spaces of their and our lives, in the places between work and projects. How can we spiritually care for others in the spaces of their lives, if we make no space for quiet and prayer in our own? Prayer in the spaces will lead to stronger spiritual energy and identity and an ever-renewing practice of spiritual care for others.

In conclusion, as a helper focused on internal healing, the spiritual caregiver must have a basic capacity for establishing a helping relationship, bring spiritual awareness into the helping relationship, and accept his or her role as a spiritual caregiver. These aptitudes and skills are needed even before a more formal spiritual assessment and care can take place. Indeed, the helper needs a sense, an outlook, and a conviction that spiritual awareness for helpees lives and grows in an atmosphere, in an environment of caring relationships. Out of such a background, the helper can enable the helpee to fulfill her or his spiritual needs for deeper meaning, connection, and hope in life. Moreover, the caregiver needs to develop a growing belief, faith in her or his role and identity as a helper who can facilitate the spiritual well-being of others. Finally, developing a meaningful spiritual image for her or his healing role together with time in quiet and prayer will greatly facilitate this spiritual identity for the caregiver.

Reflection Questions: Would you find it helpful to have a spiritual image of yourself as a caregiver? What might it be? Do you have any space in your life for prayer and self-reflection? Discuss how you might allow yourself to stop and be quiet in prayer. Do you have any particular style of prayer that enables you to do this? Do you think that calling to mind in prayer your helpees would enable you to grow in spiritual care for them?

Chapter 6

Broader Skills of Spiritual Care

Helpers need to develop a wide range of skills to adequately facilitate spiritual care. To be more inclusive, even all-inclusive, in spiritual care the helper needs to relate her or his care to the many characteristics and circumstances of helpees. We do not find spirituality in a vacuum in the sky but down on the earth in genuine people of various ethnic and cultural backgrounds. Spirituality frequently comes to the fore most strongly when people are in pain. Also, many people identify and practice their spirituality through religious traditions. Helpers need to develop broader spiritual skills in these areas.

ABILITY TO RESPOND TO THE ETHNIC HERITAGE OF HELPEES' SPIRITUALITY

Ethnic background and cultural identity are ever-present influences on how we experience life, the world, and the Spirit. To some degree our original ethnic ways still run in our veins. They are the formative and ingrained cultural mores within us. As caregivers we certainly need to be aware of their reality in regard to spirituality. It is important to recognize and acknowledge their continual internal influence and external expressions in our own and others' spiritualities.

I find that student counselors, in the beginning process of searching their ethnic heritage, frequently question its significance. They say: "My ancestors arrived two hundred years ago." "We are so diverse now. We have become part of the American melting pot." However, as they continue their search, they realize that their ethnic heritage really does influence their identities. They realize that their specific ethnic identities are their own, not simply a part of a common blend or melting pot. What a revelation as they study and reflect on their backgrounds! They had never realized how ethnicity influences their very attitudes about life and views of human nature. In many ways, their original sense of meaning, spirituality, and religious practices have come from it. Indeed, they find their first image of God and image of self in their relationship with God.

Ethnicity is more than family heirlooms or Old World recipes. It is how people look at themselves and how others look at them. In psychological terminology, it involves self-concept. We are not as self-made as we originally imagined. Our group membership is where we all began and it continues to influence us. Ethnicity is one of the key bases for establishing our personal spiritual and religious identities. For example, coming from German heritage, I began my relationship with a God who was ever-demanding and watchful of my behavior. This image of God certainly influenced my spirituality and concept of self.

To demonstrate and model the importance of ethnic heritage in spiritual care, let us look at three ethnic groups' views of God. I hope that this process will encourage readers to reflect on their ethnic backgrounds. However, my intention is not to stereotype a particular group. Rather, it is to learn about the possible spiritual and religious backgrounds/identities of helpees based on their ethnicities. To do this, I adapted Kenny's model (1980). First, I show each ethnic group's image of God; second, how this group might feel and pray to their God in the light of this image; third, the possible unforgivable sin for this group; and fourth, how this group might see itself achieving a sense of acceptance or salvation from its God. I conclude with implications based on the previous responses.

German Ethnicity

Image of God. God is seen as a stern or demanding father figure. He watches what we are doing and not doing, and can become impatient with us. This God keeps a final tally of our life's deeds. He is looking for us to get our work done, and could be seen as a distant "gotcha" God.

Prayer to God. Prayers to such a God are, "Help me to do your will; do not allow me to disappoint you; help me to be diligent, to work hard, and accomplish what I need to do." "Help me not to cry but to be strong." "Allow me to complete my tasks."

Unforgivable Sin. "Forgive me, God, when I am lazy and do not work." "I am trying to do my best." "I am sorry when I am overly emotional and not in control."

Sense of Acceptance/Salvation. The person of German background feels worthwhile as a person and accepted by God when work is completed, when he or she has done God's will. Success is "pulling oneself up by the bootstraps."

Implications for Spiritual Care. How can the spiritual caregiver move helpees of strong German background from a distant authoritarian God to a close personal loving God? With the German focus on completing tasks and work, helpees need to learn that God loves them as they are even without completing their work. The spiritual caregiver needs to enable helpees to have time to do nothing and to relax in God's love. Focus the helpees' work efforts within the context of bringing the reign of God into their world rather than simply working. God in the end brings God's reign. It is not just the helpees always working at it. Help clients to express feelings and not always the need to be in control. Success can simply mean being in or surrendering to the Presence of God.

Irish Ethnicity

Image of God. God is more a judge than a lover. However, even as a loving God, God is a jealous lover who demands full attention and service. This God speaks in terms of morality, calling people to be good. He calls for faithfulness and obedience, instilling a sense of fear in His children. He punishes His children to turn them back to the good. He calls them to suffer in this life as they serve others. Persecution, humiliation, and rejection are to be expected as part of life in this world. Offer it up to God. God is a Father who keeps the family together.

Prayer to God. "Oh God, help me to be good and to do good. Forgive my sins." "Answer my many pleas. Protect me from evil. Give me strength. Help me to persevere. Teach me your will." "Keep me loyal to you, to family, and to my faith." "Lord, have mercy on me." "The family that prays together stays together."

Unforgivable Sin. The unforgivable Irish sin is autonomy and independence, breaking away from God, family, and the church. It is most important to preserve the privacy of the family. "Shh, what will the neighbors think?" Respectability is of prime importance.

Sense of Acceptance/Salvation. For the Irish person, God loves and accepts you when you are faithful, loyal, and dedicated to His way of life found in the traditions of your family and church. If you follow the rules and live correctly, God will take care of you. Strive for perfection. "Be ye perfect as your heavenly father is perfect." It is as important to be perfect in small things as well as large. The undusted table leg is as important as not committing a serious sin.

Implications for Spiritual Care. The spiritual caregiver can help Irish clients reframe their image of God. This image of God might move from a demanding persistent God to a more gentle, loving, comforting God. Allow the real God to come alive; this God who moves us from struggles and hardships to life and resurrection. Facilitate the helpees' moving beyond Irish reliance, persistence, and determination to allow God also to lift them up and remove their fear and guilt. Hard times and difficulties are not God's punishment or merely testing. Relax and do not worry so much what other people think. God accepts us as we are.

African-American Ethnicity

Image of God. God is there for us in all our struggles, pain, and servitude. Look how He has enabled us to survive the horrors of slavery and even present persecution through racism. We can rely totally on God. God is loving and faithful. Remember in hard times that God is in charge. "What goes around, comes around." As the children of a loving Father, God may be strict and punish us at times. "Because I am His child, He corrects me." God is a sovereign God. "All praise and glory to Him."

Prayer to God. "My God, I am so grateful for all you have done for me and my ancestors, for enabling us to survive and come this far." "I am grateful to be a member of your loving family, grateful for my faith and hope in your Scriptures." "May there come a time when all races and nationalities worship your power and glory. Lord help me to survive. All praise to you."

Unforgivable Sin. For the African American, the worst sin would be to forget God, giving up and falling into hopelessness and despair. We must always remember that God is our constant deliverer.

Sense of Acceptance/Salvation. For many African Americans, people are forgiven and saved from their sins in the deliverance and the blood of Jesus. "God took my sin and gave me his righteousness. I am never good enough for this marvelous gift." "I can only receive Jesus into my heart and believe that I am saved. My role is to respond to his salvation through a good life and praising God in my life and church." "In difficult situations, I rely on the hand of God."

Implications for Spiritual Care. For African Americans, the spiritual caregiver's role in hard times is to simply draw upon the positive images of God and salvation found in their traditions. Encourage them to have the continued faith and hope in a Sovereign and Loving God who cares for them. In times of rejection, encourage them to look for the good and remember the forgiving, loving spirit of their ancestors. God is faithful to the end. Persevere in spiritual disciplines.

From these three examples, we can see the important role that helpees' original ethnic image of God and spirituality can play in their psychological and spiritual development. Bernard, a young man of German background, struggles to free himself of guilt when he is not continually working and completing his tasks. He desires to know a God of playful spirit, not just a God of work. Maureen, a middle-aged woman of Irish heritage, very much wants to feel close to a loving comforting God. Because she thinks that she is never a good-enough person, she fears a demanding God. She wonders whether she can ever feel a close communion with her God and indeed with herself. Latisha, an elderly African-American woman, experiences rejection at her mostly white senior center. She struggles to find faith in her sustaining God who can constantly raise her up in courage.

A Self-Assessment of Ethnicity and Spirituality

An excellent source to learn about many ethnic heritages is the book *Ethnicity and Family Therapy* (McGoldrick, Pearce, and Giordano, 1982). To discover the relationship of a particular ethnic group and its spirituality, ask the helpee to reflect on and answer the following questions:

1. Why do you think your ancestors came to this country? What does this say about the people they were? What legacy might you have from their struggles? (Green, 1999)
2. What might have been their core ethnic strengths and now your personal benefits? Are there any privileges you enjoy today because of your ethnic background?
3. Was their ethnic image of God passed down in your family?
4. What was your family prayer to God in light of your family's ethnic background?
5. Based on your ethnicity, what is the unforgivable sin?
6. How does someone in your ethnic group feel acceptance from the group and salvation from God?
7. Do these questions affect how you do spiritual care? How?

Answering these questions will enable helpees to be more aware of their possible early image of God and their own spirituality. Moreover, answering these questions in regard to helpees will enable the helper to be more aware of and sensitive to their ethnic spiritual roots. It will enable him or her to be a more effective spiritual caregiver.

Reflection Questions: Do you think that ethnic heritage is an important focus in spiritual care? Have you considered whether your ethnic heritage influences your spirituality and/or relationship with God? Can you see how a person's sense of self-acceptance and salvation can come from his or her image of God? How can a person heal and make more whole a psychological and spiritually unhealthy image of God? Discuss how a spiritual caregiver's ethnic background and image of God will influence how she or he does spiritual care.

ABILITY TO WORK WITH HELPEES' PAIN, LOSS, AND GRIEF

The ability to stay and be with people in pain is one of the key skills and values of a spiritual caregiver. The helper may do a thorough spiritual assessment, but without the ability to also be with people's struggles, the spiritual assessment means little. I uneasily once heard the head of a hospital's spiritual care department stereotype nuns as always positive and cheery. As such, she was concerned that as chaplains they would not be able to be with patients in pain. She feared that they would ignore the pain and attempt to help the patient feel only positive and upbeat. A friend who was in the hospital and experiencing a lot of pain spoke of how frustrated and angry he was with one particular nurse who would constantly say, "Think positive; cheer up." I share these two examples to point out how important it is for caregivers to feel pain and really empathize with the situation of the helpee. So often I find that beginning helpers think that their role is to facilitate feeling better in their helpees, to change their negative attitudes to positive ones. Hopefully, this will eventually happen through the process of solid spiritual care. However, initially, as we saw earlier, our role is to feel and be empathetic with the presenting attitudes and feelings of helpees. These initial feelings are most frequently negative and painful. Faiver et al. (2001), in their book *Explorations in Counseling and Spirituality,* even speak of "affirming the suffering" of others (p. 69).

How do people experience healing from pain in their lives and peace in their hearts? Internal healing does not happen quickly just by asking others to think positively. Rather, we heal and change and grow when people first accept us as we are in our pain and struggles. Somehow from others' caring empathy for our pain, we receive healing energy. To help others, we need to face and feel their pain with them.

The following is a hypothetical example of a beginning helpee failing to do this:

CHAPLAIN: Hello, Mr. H. My name is Chaplain John Burke, and I am part of the pastoral care team here in the hospital.

PATIENT: Hello. It's nice to meet you.

CHAPLAIN: How you are doing?

PATIENT: Well, I have a problem with my liver and I'm itchy. I'm jaundiced. Can you see how yellow my skin is?

CHAPLAIN: Yes, I can. I can see that your skin is yellow. I did not realize that you would be itchy also. (This is a good response as the chaplain acknowledges the helpee's present condition.)

PATIENT: Yes, it's very itchy. It has something to do with the bile backing up. The doctor says that I have cancer. I am going to be operated on Tuesday.

CHAPLAIN: Oh, I will come on Tuesday and pray for you especially.

Although it is good to pray, the chaplain's response did not touch into the pain of the helpee by acknowledging the fear of cancer. Perhaps the helper could not face the pain of the helpee's cancer, so he avoided it by talking about prayer. A better response would have been, "You have cancer and you are anxiously waiting for the operation on Tuesday."

PATIENT: Thank you. I believe in the power of prayer. Prayers are important. I would also like to talk about the fact that I have cancer.

CHAPLAIN: I think it is good that we can bring it out into the open. It helps when you can talk about something.

Once again, the helper ignores the helpee's concerns and anxiety over cancer. The chaplain talks in general terms about how good it is to talk about it in the open. Yet the chaplain does not openly respond to the helpee's fear, or even to mention cancer. A better response for the chaplain would be, "So you really want to talk about your cancer. Can I help you with this?" Perhaps the chaplain was afraid of the helpee's anger or deep sadness that might arise if the chaplain opened up a conversation around the cancer.

Carl Rogers (1942) in his lifelong goal and work to help people find effective ways to change and grow, describes characteristic steps in the helping process. One of the initial steps is that the helper encourage free expression of painful or even negative feelings in regard to a helpee's problem. To do this, the helper might use an open-ended question such as, "How do you feel today?" In response initially, a helpee with a problem usually expresses negative or painful feelings. The helper must not deflect, ignore, or deny the helpee's painful feelings. Rather the helper "accepts, recognizes, and clarifies these negative feelings" (p. 37). If the helper has the energy and ability to stay with the helpee's expression of negative feelings, eventually the helper will begin to hear the helpee tentatively move toward the positive. For instance, the helpee may eventually respond, "Well, the situation is not completely bad." Such a tentative positive response shows that growth and deeper healing are taking place. The helper at this point can continue facilitating this positive growth. The question that the helper asks self in this whole process is: Can she or he sit with or listen to the pain long enough to allow the helpee to work through it to some healing and deeper spiritual connection?

With the previous case of Mr. H., the patient with cancer, if the chaplain had responded to and stayed with Mr. H.'s fears of cancer rather than evading it, the patient could have experienced the possibility of working through the fear. Mr. H. might have moved through the fear to some beginning statements of hope such as, "I am doing everything that I can. I have good doctors. I place my trust in God and hope for the best. God has always been with me in the past. Why should it be different now? My life here is not over yet. I'll wait and see what happens in the operation." This ability to work with a helpee's fears and pain is a key skill for the spiritual caregiver. We need not take away or ignore other people's pain, but we can help them work through it. It is always best to go through a problem rather than around it.

Frequently in spiritual care, problems arise that are not going to go away, such as the loss of a loved one or a terminal illness. Such pain calls out for a deeper spiritual connection, an expanded sense of meaning, forgiveness, and hope. For example, if a patient with cancer finds out that the cancer is inoperable, will the patient be able to grow and find a deeper connection in loss other than connection with a healthy life?

Moreover, loss with the corresponding need for deeper spiritual connection is found in all problems, not only in major death and life issues. For example, people of racial or sexual minorities may grieve the loss of common acceptance. They need to move deeper spiritually to find God's acceptance and a broader meaning to their lives. Through examining their beliefs and spiritual experiences, they can find strength and even serenity. Spiritual care for them may be to know that nothing can separate them from the love of God. With spirituality, the helpee can continue to receive God's love in all situations and, in return, to give love to others.

Spirituality enables us to transcend the limited physical and psychological views of pain and loss. We develop inner harmony and deeper and broader interconnections. We can experience spiritual well-being even in the midst of pain and loss.

Other pain might be from loneliness, job loss, hospitalization, or family and relationship difficulties. In loneliness, we feel at a loss for closeness to others. Spirituality can bring companionship and community. In hospitalization, we lose our freedom, privacy, and even our health. Spirituality can bring inner healing and some peace. In job loss we lose our livelihood and even some of our self-esteem. Spirituality can bring meaning and hope in this situation. In family or relationship difficulties, we grieve the loss of harmony and closer community. Spirituality can bring forgiveness and healing here.

Spirituality also brings strength and courage to everyday ordinary pains and disappointments. These might be disappointment in a friend, feeling too tired to complete our work, or forgetting to do what we promised. Through deeper grounding and creating wider perspectives in everyday life situations, our spirituality sustains and further enlivens us. Indeed, in all life situations, spirituality and spiritual care can bring us healing and hope.

The spiritual caregiver is not a romantic idealist simplistically and naively turning pain and struggles over to a Higher Power. Spiritual caregivers know that we never really escape from struggles and problems; the next problem is just around the corner. Life is a continuous struggle with pains and losses. However, in spirituality people can ground their lives and learn how to grieve losses as they appear. A spiritual caregiver grieves well and teaches and helps others find the healthy freedom of doing the same. Through the process of grief and letting go, a person moves forward. The difference between the spiritual and nonspiritual focus of helping is the realization through spirituality that our egos are not soundly in control of life. In reality, we are not in control or all powerful. We are part of a process much larger than we are or can imagine. We seek deeper connections with this process, with the unity of the universe, with the flow of life, with our God. By following the path of spiritual well-being in hope and inner harmony, we can realistically become aware of and sensitive to the pains and struggles of our lives.

Reflection Questions: As a spiritual caregiver, are you able to listen to pain and sit with it? Can you hear painful feelings even when they are not expressed? Can you verbally acknowledge them or do you go around them? Do you experience the process of helping another as standing with and moving through pain to deeper connections and meaning? Can you share an example of when someone has really helped you in struggles and pain? Did this take place through the helper going around your pain or through acknowledging and feeling your hurt with you? What hurts and losses do the people that you serve experience? How does their spirituality and your spiritual care facilitate spiritual healing and even a sense of spiritual wellness?

ABILITY TO UTILIZE HELPEES' BELIEFS

The Faith Factor

Religious caregivers who already use their helpees' religious beliefs and practices in their helping roles may find it redundant to speak of this skill. However, as stated in the preface, Pruyser (1976), a psychologist from the Menninger Clinic who worked with chaplains, was disappointed that many were not effectively using their patients' religious beliefs in their pastoral care work. He encouraged them to make optimal use of their helpees' theology as well as their psychology. In addition to this piece of information, psychological professionals in general share a long history of viewing religious beliefs as frequently detrimental or just not important to psychological well-being. As a result, they may fear and ignore them in their helping.

Moreover, modern society mostly consigns religion to the private sphere of life and hence counselors do not easily and readily refer to it. Recently, researchers, concerned with this lack, have spoken of the "religious commitment gap" (Larson and Larson, 1994). They examine the gap between the large number of Americans who believe in God and find religion important in their lives versus the much smaller percentage of psychiatrists and psychologists who find religion important or even useful in treatment. A 1993 Gallup poll (Princeton Religious Research Center, 1993) showed that 96 percent of Americans believed in God; moreover, 66 percent considered religion to be most important or very important in their lives. However, Jensen and Bergin's study (1988) showed that only 29 percent of therapists saw religious content as important in treatment. As the statistics show, for many helpees, religious experience is an important part of their human experience.

The tide is changing. An increasing number of medical and mental health professionals (Koenig, 1997, 1999; Koenig, McCullough, and Larson, 2001) are beginning to speak of the "faith factor" in physical and mental health. They are looking at the possible health benefits for people who are religious. For example, Propst and colleagues (1992) found that in therapy depressed patients receiving treatment involving religious content did better than patients with whom religious content was omitted. The relationship between religion or faith and health is an important one for spiritual caregivers. It shows how vital and effective the use of religious belief in spiritual care can be for helpees' physical and mental health, let alone their spiritual health. Several studies (Larson and Larson, 1994) have shown the positive relationship between religious commitment and mortality (how long we live), morbidity (getting particular diseases), and cardiovascular disease. Religious commitment also positively influences health (Larson and Larson, 1991).

We learned earlier that helpees' spirituality or religion can be brought into conversation through the use of open-ended questions. For example, "Mrs. Smith, do you follow a religious or spiritual path? What is it saying to you in your present situation?" We can both communicate openness to the use of religion in the healing process and also show a nonjudgmental acceptance of a helpee's particular religious beliefs and practices. Experiencing this, Mrs. Smith may respond that her religion gives her hope in God's care at this time. Or she may respond that she is angry with God for her present situation and questions God's goodness and even existence. She may respond that she feels guilty for something in her past and she thinks that God is punishing her with the present sickness or pain. From any of these responses the spiritual caregiver could begin the process of reframing and clarifying the helpee's religion as part of the process of healing spiritual care.

Supportive Attitudes Toward Other Religions

As we use helpees' religious beliefs and traditions, we need to have a strong attitude of respecting and even treasuring and celebrating them. One way to begin this is simply to show a healthy interest in the helpees' religions. We may not be familiar with it, but we can ask them to share and explain the beliefs and practices that relate to their present situations. Religion in our present culture is viewed as a very private matter. Religious beliefs are perhaps the most intimate part of a person's personality. However, in a gentle and sensitive way, we can inquire and ask for some clarification in the religious or spiritual area just as we do in helping people in other areas of their lives. For example, in working with a helpee who follows New Age spirituality, I would want to understand the person's view of the world and how she or he comes to spiritual healing and wellness.

Our attitude toward other religions is of prime importance. If we follow a particular religious path that is very meaningful to us, a path that has helped us in our life's joys and struggles, we may want to share this with others. The person may even ask us to do so. However, our role is first to be with the helpee in his or her religion and its spirituality, not to proselytize or impose our own religious convictions (Association for Clinical Pastoral Education, Inc., 2001). Only when we allow ourselves to be aware that we may want to proselytize can we stop ourselves from doing so. Because of centuries of religious disputes, religious issues may indeed live, if not in our conscious minds at least in our subconscious. We need to become more aware of our own religious issues (Kelly, 1995), or for that matter an issue with religion itself. Otherwise, these issues get in the way of our working with people of various religious beliefs.

For instance, in working with the person from a New Age spirituality perspective, I need to be aware of my own bias or stereotype that followers of New Age philosophy view the world always from the positive and are not aware enough of evil in the world. In such a situation, I would inquire about how my helpee with New Age spirituality views the world. I would sensitively state where I am coming from. Otherwise, as a helper, I would be fearful that I could subtly and unethically influence the helpee.

We very naturally do spiritual care out of our own religious or spiritual background. We have to work to expand beyond our own views of the spiritual world. I once supervised a group of students who had a very difficult time bringing themselves to say a Catholic "Hail Mary" with Catholic helpees. It was almost against their religion to do such a thing. Likewise, a Catholic helper may need to stretch himself or herself to do more spiritual care out of a scriptural base as well as a sacramental, ritual focus. Through clarification of helpers' own ideas in relationship to their own beliefs, the spiritual growth of helpees is likely to proceed in a more free and open manner. As caregivers, we constantly strive for increasing openness to the riches of the world's religions and spiritualities.

Interspirituality

Wayne Teasdale (1999) speaks of celebrating a unifying spirituality underlying and connecting all our diverse religious beliefs and practices. He calls this movement "interspirituality" and hopes that religions are moving toward it. He speaks of spirituality as the world's first religion. All peoples have shared a spiritual quest for transcendence, and out of this quest arose our diverse religious traditions. We all share spirituality. As humans, we are spiritually interdependent. It might be very worthwhile to think of ourselves and our helpees' shared spirituality as we work within the differences and diversities of their religious faiths and practices. Our religious beliefs coalesce in spirit and unite through spirituality. Spirituality is our common source. Interspirituality is the "essential spiritual interdependence of the [world's] religions" (p. 27).

The model of spiritual needs and care developed in this book is a beginning attempt to practice interspirituality and bring more connection among many religions. Through an identification of common shared spiritual needs of all people, we can do spiritual care in many religious traditions. We speak of four spiritual needs—the need for meaning, the need to give love, the need to receive love, and the need for forgiveness, hope, and creativity. As we work with helpees of any religious tradition, we can assess for ourselves and with them how their religious beliefs and practices give meaning, love and connection, forgiveness and hope. How can I as a spiritual caregiver use helpees' religious traditions to help fulfill their core spiritual needs, a sense of forgiveness, hope, wholeness, and spiritual wellness? The Christian helpee may find meaning and spiritual growth in the love of Jesus, the Jewish helpee in the practice of Shabbat, the Buddhist in meditative unity with the cosmos. The beliefs and practices are varied. The spirituality of growing in meaning is universal. It is one.

As spiritual caregivers, we desire to enable our helpees to uncover, to discover, and many times even to recover the spirituality and the

spiritual riches in their religious traditions. For us personally as helpers, it is rewarding to work with helpees with so many rich religious
traditions. We most probably find ourselves rooted in one tradition. It
is part of our very identity. We celebrate this. We primarily live and
grow in this tradition, and we may spiritually think and do most of our
spiritual care out of it. However, this does not mean that we are stuck
only in our one tradition (Teasdale, 1999). The Spirit enriches many
traditions. The question for us is how to learn and feel more comfort-
able in other traditions. We do this knowing that to really learn the beliefs and practices of all religious traditions is impossible. However,
we can focus our search on the interspirituality lived in each tradition
and discover how its traditions and beliefs fulfill our basic spiritual
needs. The following is a paradigm of how three monotheistic religions share an interspirituality that fulfills basic spiritual needs.

Islam

Sense of Meaning. Meaning and fulfillment are found in belief and
acceptance of the One God with Muhammad as his prophet. We are
happy when we live the divine will through our particular role in every area of our lives. Faith is the key virtue. The "one and only purpose in life should be constantly to seek and to do what is acceptable
to God" (Al-Tantawi, 1997, p. 31).

Sense of Love and Deep Connection. We are deeply connected
with our God and with our Muslim brothers and sisters in our five
daily times of prayer. To be aware of God's presence brings much
love and community. The cultivation of virtue leads to heaven. We
feel cared for and receive blessings through following the Holy
Quran and the hadith's total scheme for living. Our faith is practical,
based on the realities of life.

Sense of Forgiveness and Hope. God forgives provided we repent
and ask for forgiveness. We seek refuge in prayer and are constantly
purified through our prayer. Moreover, our prayer saves us from evil.
Especially in the season of Ramadan, we receive hope through our
fasting and almsgiving. We constantly hope in God and His ways. He
has laid down the laws of nature that we follow. God fulfills our needs
(Altareb, 1996).

Christianity

Sense of Meaning. Meaning is found in living in union with the Trinity—God the Creator, God the Son, and God the Holy Spirit. God the Creator redeems and accepts us through the Son, Christ Jesus. Because of the Son's redemption, we can now live in the healing love of the Holy Spirit. Through our exemplary lives in this world, we bring forth the reign of God in preparation for Christ coming again.

Sense of Love and Deep Connection. We can have a personal relationship with an all-powerful and all-loving God in prayer. We draw close to our neighbor through service. In gratitude, we worship our God and find support in a caring Christian community. We receive love through loving others. We live in awe of God's goodness through creation and through the love and care of fellow human beings.

Sense of Forgiveness and Hope. Our sins are forgiven through the redeeming healing power of Christ's death. God constantly reaches out to us with this forgiving love. We have but to repent and ask for forgiveness. We have a solid hope in the redemption of Christ and a God who loves (Richards and Bergin, 1997; Smith, 1991).

Judaism

Sense of Meaning. Meaning is found in belief and love of the one God and especially in doing the traditional rituals carried out in families. We find our meaning in being part of God's chosen people. We pass on our heritage with its rituals, values, and traditions to our children.

Sense of Love and Deep Connection. Our culture with its laws and customs makes us one, especially through all the persecution in the past and even in the present. Ours is a way of life, not just a belief. Because of our oppression, we look to help other oppressed peoples. We value learning of the one God and all learning. All God made is good. We enjoy the legitimate pleasures of this world, including our sexuality, as paths to spiritual fulfillment.

Sense of Forgiveness and Hope. The one God made the world good, including our very selves. We may do wrong, but we do have free will to choose a moral life. We have hope that we can overcome evil. Life is treasured as a gift from God. God gives us hope (Grollman, 1990).

These are certainly only beginning examples attempting to show an interspirituality between Islam, Christianity, and Judaism. I am sure that you can build on them as you work with your helpees' spiritual needs in the area of transcendent meaning, giving and receiving love with its need for connection, and finally in their need for healing, forgiveness, and hope. Countless religious denominations share an interspiritual path. Each religion or way of life in its own beliefs and practices brings meaning, transcendence, love, connectedness, forgiveness, and hope. For the reader interested in brief religious summaries of many denominations' beliefs and practices, Christian and non-Christian, see Smith (1991), Kelly (1995), and Carpenito (1997).

Working with Helpees' Theological Concepts

To work effectively with religiously oriented helpees, we need a feel for and a basic knowledge of some key theological terms. This so-called "God language" may frighten secular professionals into thinking they do not know any of that dogma. They may wonder how useful it could be to helpees. Note here that I am not talking about the substance of articles of faith or interpretations of dogma. Rather, I am speaking of the functional use of theological concepts or words of faith that helpees use to speak not just of their religious experiences but even of their human experiences of life. For example, a helpee may speak of sin or grace in regard to what is taking place in the world and even his or her own life. As helpers interested in spiritual care, we do not have to know how to recite a creed, but we do need to empathize with our helpees' theological or religious perspectives.

Pruyser (1976) lists some key theological concepts that religious helpees might well use. They include understanding or concept of God, sense of sin, capacity for faith, conception of salvation, faith support system, and sense of hope.

Kathleen Norris (1998), in her popular book *Amazing Grace,* takes similar theological terms, calls them "a vocabulary of faith," and relates them to life experiences. She explains how these key theological concepts really influence many people's lives for good or for ill, depending on how they understand and live them. However, as she points out so well in her book, if we really look at even the "scariest" theological concepts and healthily reframe them, we can use them in our psychological and spiritual care. As such, these theological terms can become strong sources for spiritual wellness.

Working with a healthy understanding of God can bring much meaning and healing, and can sustain a person's life. Looking at sin not so much from a guilty conscience but from what stands in our way of spiritual growth and union with God can bring a need for healthy change in our lives. Determining helpees' capacity for faith points out their ability to make deep spiritual connections with what lies beyond themselves. Their concepts of salvation tell us how they view God's acceptance and deliverance. They tell us how they feel about themselves and how they find internal forgiveness and hope.

To one person, salvation may mean Christ saving humanity from sin and each person being born again in the death and resurrection of Christ. To another person, it may mean liberation from sickness and illness; to another, it may mean changing societal structures to bring freedom and self-actualization; finally, to another it may simply mean being freed from a terrible situation such as an unfulfilling job or chaotic legal problems. Working with helpees in a faith support system may enable them to grow in receiving and giving love in a community context.

Finally, assessing helpees' sense of hope enables them to realize how creative their lives can be. Our lived or functional theological vocabularies reveal to us our spirituality and focus of spiritual wellness. The spiritual power of healthily reframed theological concepts is amazing. Perhaps that is why Norris titled her book about a modern clarification of theological terms *Amazing Grace.*

Reflection Questions: In regard to the "faith factor," what relationship have you experienced or seen between beliefs, including religious belief and health? How might some individual unhealthy religious beliefs be reinterpreted or reframed in a healthy way? Can you develop supportive attitudes toward religious beliefs other than your own? What might they be? What are some common spiritual themes and paths that unite all religious paths? Can you find the basic four spiritual needs in various religious beliefs? What are your helpees' vocabularies of faith? Do they use any of the theological terms that were discussed in this chapter? Usually they are not spoken; however, can you recognize any key theological themes in their life stories? How do you feel about Pruyser's theological terms for yourself?

What is your lived experience of these theological concepts? Do they speak to your sense of spiritual growth and wellness?

ABILITY TO USE RELIGIOUS RESOURCES

At times, spiritual caregivers can appropriately and effectively bring resources from religious traditions such as symbol and ritual into the helping relationship. As a result of spirituality's evolution into many belief traditions throughout the centuries, religions have developed many meaningful symbols and rituals to facilitate transcendent connection and healing. A significant part of spiritual care can be the use of these religious resources, symbols, and rituals within the helping relationship. For example, although in the Jewish tradition we see an important part of spiritual care focusing on sharing wisdom and truth, we also see the use of many rich symbols and rituals in the home and synagogue such as candles and Torah. In the Catholic Christian tradition, religious resources such as Mass and the sacraments are frequently the main focus of spiritual care. In the Protestant Christian tradition, the book of Scriptures is probably the main source of spiritual care.

Present-day psychologists and counselors are also looking more seriously at ritual and symbols as instruments of healing and care. Look at the present emphasis on the use of ritual in family therapy. Here therapist and counselee develop and carry out a personalized ritual to symbolize healing in family relationships, to mark important transitions, or to celebrate an achievement. Also, counselors at times may employ a spiritual or religious resource such as meditation or prayer. They can encourage helpees to use the religious resources of their traditions that give to them special meaning and comfort in their problems. As Jung states: "Everything to do with religion, everything it is and asserts, touches the human soul so closely that psychology least of all can afford to overlook it" (cited in Jacobi and Hull, 1970, p. 359).

Spiritual care calls for more than an intellectual or psychological relationship. We may indeed think of spiritual care mostly in a psychological way of identifying and working with people's spiritual needs. Spiritual care, however, is not always just conversation and listening in a helping relationship. If so, spiritual care can become overly intellectual and too verbal, not engaging the whole person's senses and unconscious. In this way, we would greatly limit the practice of spiritual care. At times it can call for a deeper connection to the Divine through the use of religious resources. As spiritual caregivers, we help others move toward transcendent meaning in their life experiences. In this process, we become more aware that we stand on holy ground with them and live in a sacred space. Religious resources, rituals, and symbols can put our helpees in touch with this holy ground. In them they can experience the numinous or the sacred that can bring healing energy. Theologically, we might call this experience "grace." Examples of religious resources might be meditation, prayer, sacraments, music, art, and various religious symbols and materials.

Spiritual care for many people includes both the psychological help of identifying spiritual needs in words and conversation and also the spiritual help of religious resources. Various religious traditions may favor one over the other, the verbal over the ritual and symbol, or the ritual and symbol over the verbal. Holistic care of the person can look to both. Today there is a strong need for better integration, not placing one or the other on the periphery or making the one an addendum to the other. Certainly, religious helpers already regularly draw on the religious resources of their traditions, such as prayer, music, the scriptures, symbols, ceremonies, and sacramental rituals. For many people in faith traditions, ritual and other religious resources are the focus of their spiritual healing and growth. "Throughout the world, ritualized devotion is the most popular way to make contact with the divine" (George, 2000, p. 112). The regular church member can find sustenance, healing, guidance, and reconciliation from scriptures, ceremonies, symbols, and sacramental actions. Universally, religions use symbols and rituals at key points in life such as birth, initiation into adulthood, commitments, death, and times of needed healing. The following are some of the key religious resources from the Christian, Islamic, and Jewish traditions.

Christianity's Healing Symbols and Rituals

- Prayer and meditation, use of blessings
- The Bible, prayer books, and hymnals
- Sacraments of Initiation, Communion (Celebration of the Eucharist), Reconciliation, Anointing of the Sick

- The laying on of hands, group prayer for healing
- Use of religious articles such as candles, holy water, etc.

Islam's Healing Symbols and Rituals

- Prayer five times a day
- Group prayer for healing
- Faith in the Holy Quran and other revealed books
- The season of Ramadan
- Fasting during Ramadan

Judaism's Healing Symbols and Rituals

- Prayer and meditation
- Ritual circumcision
- Burial ritual of washing the body
- The Torah and Talmud
- Holy days
- Fasting during certain holy days
- Use of religious articles such as candles, menorah, Star of David, etc.

Some people in their minds and hearts may separate religious ritual from spirituality. They fear that religious rituals repeated over and over again become meaningless, leaving a spiritual void. We know that this can and does happen. A person can thoughtlessly say the words or automatically perform ritual actions without any spiritual awareness. However, rituals do not have to be carried out without spiritual awareness. They can be carried out with meaning and bring the Divine into our lives. They can make the Spirit available to us.

The psychologist Carl Jung (1961) pointed out that symbols and rituals have the awesome possibility of connecting us with the depth of our being's inner-healing energy. They can be spiritually effective by themselves, even without words. Symbols and rituals can reach beyond our conscious minds, deep into our hearts and unconscious. They can convey the healing energy that they symbolize. For instance, Jung states that just devotedly looking at a religious symbol, such as a cross, can give the participant internal spiritual energy. He grieves the loss of many religious symbols over the past several centuries. Indeed, he views symbols and rituals as bringing emotional healing for the common person down through the ages. In a sense they were the poor peasant's therapy. He states, "Charged with archetypal power, symbols introduce the zest of divine into consciousness, turning every human life into a spiritual adventure of meaning" (Jung, 1961, p. 131). Meaning is the key word here. Religious symbols convey a deeper meaning and resultant connection that leads to spiritual healing and health. They accomplish this by bringing to the helpee an experience of unity, a sense of divinity. For example, in the Christian Anointing of the Sick with holy oil, the symbol of the oil can bring the deeper meaning and experience of healing of body and soul for the sick person. The person's body may not be healed, but the symbolic ritual facilitates a unity with divinity and resultant strong inner peace of the soul and whole.

Symbols and rituals can unfold the sacredness of spiritual care. They enliven the sacred place within us and make transcendent meaning more concrete and alive. Spirituality becomes a sacred experience symbolized in ritual action. Thus, symbols transform energy by facilitating new and higher forms of unconscious activity. In this way, they do spiritual care. As such, spiritual care becomes more than guidance. It becomes healing, sustenance, and reconciliation. For example, reflect on the use of the Scriptures, the word of God in spiritual care. The symbol of the Holy Book becomes the reality of God's words spoken for healing consolation and challenge to the helpee. These words put the helpee in closer union with God, the transcendental loving source of spiritual care and growth. They give the helpee sustenance and can even lead to forgiveness and reconciliation. The Holy Book symbolizes God's life reaching out to the world.

Spiritual care is more than a helping relationship. It is a relationship of presence—presence of the sacred. Rituals and symbols create this presence of spirit. Sacramental and other ritual spiritual care done with soul and reverence convey a strong spiritual healing presence (see Willimon, 1979). For example, in many Christian traditions the celebration of the sacrament of Reconciliation can bring peace and hope to a wounded heart that has not experienced it for years. The symbol of the sacrament conveys a powerful spiritual presence that brings healing without many words, without much guidance, though guidance may follow. Of course, for spiritual caregivers who employ religious rituals and resources, it is important to carry rituals out in this spirit of sacred presence. To do this, we need a place of quiet presence within ourselves. We need to experience the sacred within in order to convey it in the ritual and to touch the sacred in our helpees. For caregivers, this spirit can come out of our own times of prayer, quiet, and meditation. The Spirit comes alive in silence. Out of our own contemplation, the Spirit brings us to an appreciation of the sacred in our heart, in the world and its religious paths, in our helpees, and in our God. This beautiful appreciation and reverence of symbol and ritual takes us to sacred spaces and places. We enjoy the feel of being in and handling the sacred. Spiritual care through the integrated use of religious resources such as symbols and rituals can lead to a healthier holistic care of the person.

Reflection Questions: How do you feel about the possible use of ritual and religious resources in the helping relationship? Is ritual only ritual or does it have meaning for you? What religious symbols and rituals bring spiritual meaning to you and your helpees? Do you attempt to be in touch with the meaning and sacredness of your helpees' religious resources? Can you celebrate the many religions and their prayers, symbols, and rituals? Although they have different symbols and rituals, can you see the spiritual lake that supplies them all? Where do you experience the sacred? Does any past religious or spiritual experience still bring you spiritual energy? How do you feel about silence? Do you ever have a sense of a spiritual presence as you counsel or facilitate the spiritual care of others?

Chapter 7

A Community Model of Spiritual Care

ABILITY TO DEVELOP A SOCIALLY RESPONSIBLE FOCUS IN SPIRITUAL CARE

Because of the psychological one-on-one focus of helping, care-givers can easily neglect and ignore the social focus of spiritual care. Spirituality is frequently seen as the part of the person that is personal and private, a personal piety. Spiritual people are sometimes stereo-typed as not involved in the affairs of this world (Doran, 1984). For many, social responsibility and justice are usually not associated with spirituality. Spirituality is seen as interior holiness, and justice is looked upon as an external practice concerned with changing society. People live their spirituality. How does their spirituality relate to a concern for or even an advocacy for social justice? Of course, people have responsibilities to society and their neighbors. We are God's hands in the world. However, our focus is usually individuals helping other individuals rather than changing environments and systems that greatly affect the spiritual health of individual lives. Our nineteenth-century personal style of spirituality sees justice mostly as individual acts. However, the way in which the structures of our society and world affect gender, class, sexuality, race, and health really matters in spiritual care. As such, we need to expand the focus of our spiritual care beyond the individual helping relationship into social structures and systems. We need to facilitate better societal structures, which fa-cilitate spiritual health as part of whole-person health care.

A healthy spirituality focuses not only on the individual but also on the world, on all people. It is frequently said in the Roman Catholic community that its social justice teachings are its best-kept secrets. Locally, I remember the questions surrounding the founding of a cen-ter for spiritual direction. One of the main discussions at the time was whether the people who came to this center for spiritual direction would be concerned only with their own interior holiness and relationship with God. The fear was that a very personal spiritual search would take them away from the world rather than lead them back into the world to serve. However, after twenty years of experience, this center now sees many of its former and present clients compassionately serving in many causes of social justice. A sense of social justice grows out of a strong spirituality. Spirituality and justice are one.

What may be forgotten or ignored in spiritual caregiving is that helpees are part of a much larger system of care or lack of care. The context of personal spiritual care needs to expand to influence these larger structures and systems. If the structures of society and culture do not support the basic needs of many of our people for food, shelter, health, and equality, how can their spiritual needs be met? Furthermore, spirituality is the integrating piece of the whole health of a person. Benjamin and Looby (1998), citing Hettler (1979), see wellness along six major dimensions: physical, emotional, mental, social, occupational, and spiritual. They all go together. We need to be concerned about the first five dimensions as well as the sixth, the spiritual. In this book, we have viewed spiritual care as fulfilling helpee's spiritual needs for meaning, connection and love, forgiveness, and hope. How can these spiritual needs birth and grow without the basics of life: clean air and water, food and shelter, and a healthy social environment? Maslow's (1968) hierarchy of needs shows how people need first to have basic human needs met (such as food, shelter, security, a sense of belonging, and self-esteem) before the transcendent needs of the person can also grow and thrive.

Figure 7.1 shows how the world around helpees strongly affects their spiritual health. The physical, psychological, and social environments greatly determine their sense of self. People receive their sense of self-worth, feelings of safety and security, fulfillment of physical needs, and personal health from their environment. Moreover, in their world environment, people experience or do not experience a sense of community support and affirmation together with the ability to transcend and move beyond the self. Fulfilling these physical, psychological, and social needs determines helpees' abilities to fulfill their spiritual needs. The positive interaction of personal needs with their physical, psychological, and social environments enables spiritual awareness and health.

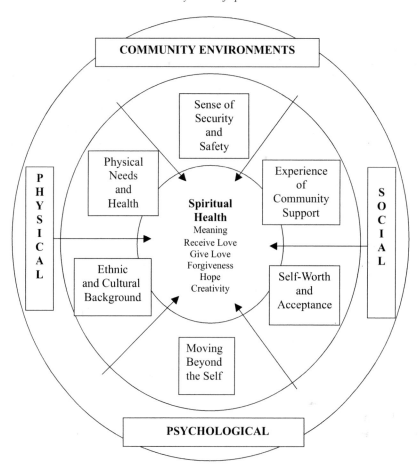

Spiritual health is centered in community care. May we
all enjoy the above circumferences in healthy measure.

FIGURE 7.1. Community Influences on Spiritual Health

As spiritual caregivers, we work and struggle to change the systems of our society that keep large numbers of people from food,
health, a secure place to live, and equality for all. Spiritual caregivers
also help others understand and act upon issues of social justice. They
encourage people to relate their spirituality/religion to the systems
that they live in. The structures of our society provide care for some
people and not for others. They are frequently "geared to the success

of the majority and the failure of the minority" (National Conference of Catholic Bishops, 1979, p. 3). We see this in the lack of health insurance and needed preventive health care for a large number of our fellow citizens. The possibilities of a good education or the ability to purchase a house in a safe neighborhood are givens to certain groups of people but not to others. We will continue to be part of the problem until we are part of the solution. We need to see spiritual care as including advocacy to change systems that kill the spirit as well as the physical health of helpees.

A COMMUNITY MODEL OF SPIRITUAL CARE

How can a community agency model a system of spiritual care whereby all peoples' spirits are fed and celebrated? Based on and adapted from a community counseling and helping model by Lewis et al. (1998), I would envision four distinct spiritual outreach activities of a community agency, two activities with an individual focus and two activities with a group-services focus:

1. Direct individual spiritual care services as presently done.
2. Indirect individual spiritual care through support and advocacy in the community for helpees' physical, emotional, and spiritual health needs.
3. Direct group services that include spirituality in such areas as addiction services, parenting groups, etc.
4. Indirect group spiritual care through advocating to change societal systems and laws that keep certain groups of people's spirit down.

This model of community spiritual care would look similar to the following:

Individual Services	**Group Services**
Direct one-on-one spiritual caregiving	Direct group programs integrating spirituality
Individual helpee advocacy	Advocacy for change of societal systems that oppress the spirit

This model expands spiritual care into the community and the structures of society that deeply affect the health and spiritual growth of our helpees. Practically speaking, we advocate for change through involvement in the political and legislative process. We need to know that our voices make a difference. We need to learn about the legislative process, stay informed, and pool resources with our colleagues in spiritual care. Do we even know our congressperson's voting record? Do we communicate on a regular basis with our legislators both at the state and federal level? Have we identified ourselves as caregivers and also made known to our legislators the needs of the helpees that we serve? To begin this process for you at the state level, contact <www.state.[two-letter abbreviation of your state].us>. For example, the Connecticut address would be <www.state.ct.us>. Here you will view your legislators' names and addresses and possibly their voting records. At the federal level, contact <http://thomas.loc.gov>. You might also contact the International Pastoral Care Network for Social Responsibility at <www.ipcnsr.org>.

Reflection Questions: Do you see the interconnectedness of spirituality, spiritual care, and social justice? What do you think of this model of community spiritual care? Can you move the context of spiritual care from an individual to a communal focus? What are the needs of your helpees and how might the structures of society help or hinder their spiritual needs? Do you have the energy and courage to be an advocate for social justice for your helpees? How can you broaden spiritual care in your organization to include a community focus?

SPIRITUAL CARE COMPETENCIES OF PROFESSIONAL ORGANIZATIONS

To conclude our discussion of the skills of the spiritual care practitioner, let us now also briefly review the spirituality competencies developed by several counseling and pastoral/spiritual care organizations. Looking at these needed competencies can reinforce what readers have learned and further specify the skills of spiritual care. Also, reviewing them can give you some guidelines for developing your own list of competencies for your spiritual care organization.

They also can personally facilitate the identification of spirituality skills that you want to further develop.

The Center for the Accreditation of Counseling and Related Education Programs (CACREP) strongly supports the role of spirituality in modern-day counseling. In the glossary section of its 2001 Standards, CACREP describes spirituality as "the inner life of that individual that is part of the wholeness of a person. Spirituality is often considered a motivating force for an individual's actions and thought processes and, therefore, may be an appropriate aspect of counseling" (<http://www.counseling.org/cacrep/>, 2001). Further, at a gathering titled a "Summit on Spirituality," this accrediting agency under its ASERVIC division—the Association for Spiritual, Ethical, and Religious Values in Counseling (Burke, 2000)—developed the following nine standards of skills or competencies needed by the counselor to work with spirituality:

> In order to be competent to help clients address the spiritual dimension of their lives, a counselor needs to be able to 1) explain the relationship between religion and spirituality, including similarities and differences, 2) describe religious and spiritual beliefs and practices in a cultural context, 3) engage in self-exploration of his/her religious and spiritual beliefs in order to increase sensitivity, understanding and acceptance of his/her belief system, 4) describe one's religious and/or spiritual belief system and explain various models of religious/spiritual development across the lifespan, 5) demonstrate sensitivity to and acceptance of a variety of religious and/or spiritual expressions in the client's communication, 6) identify the limits of one's understanding of a client's spiritual expression, and demonstrate appropriate referral skills and general possible referral sources, 7) assess the relevance of the spiritual domains in the client's therapeutic issues, 8) be sensitive to and respectful of the spiritual themes in the counseling process as befits each client's expressed preference, and 9) use a client's spiritual beliefs in the pursuit of the client's therapeutic goals as befits the client's expressed preference. (Burke, 2000, p. 2, reproduced by permission of CACREP)

The Association of Professional Chaplains lists the following key spiritual values as part of its mission and vision statement:

In promoting the mission of the Association, the following values underlie all organizational efforts:

1. The individual person possesses dignity and worth.
2. The spiritual dimension of a person is an essential part of an individual's striving for health and meaning in life.
3. The spiritual care of persons is a critical aspect of the total care offered in the delivery of care for public and private institutions and organizations.
4. Inclusivity and diversity are seen as foundational value in pastoral services offered to persons, regardless of religion, race, ethnicity, sexual orientation, age, disability or gender. Inclusivity and diversity are also valued throughout the structures of the Association.
5. Public advocacy, related to spiritual values and social justice concerns, is promoted in behalf of persons in need. ("About APC, Mission/Vision/Values," The Association of Professional Chaplains, <http://www.professionalchaplains. org/index1. html>. Reprinted by permission of the Association of Professional Chaplains.)

The National Association of Catholic Chaplains, in its 2001 "Standards for Certification of Chaplains," lists many specific competencies in the area of pastoral/spiritual care (original standard numbers are included):

410.3211. Ability to use spiritual assessment, planning, intervention, and evaluation in a clinical setting.

410.3212. Ability to understand and help others discover meaning in the experiences of suffering, grief, and loss.

410.3213. Understanding of the ways in which psychosocial dynamics and cultural/ethnic differences affect pastoral care practices.

410.3214. Ability to provide intensive and extensive pastoral care to persons of various life situations and crisis circumstances.

410.3215. Demonstrated aptitude for integrating pastoral theology with pastoral practice.

410.3216. Evidence of ability to assist and support others in the application of their own values in decision making.

410.3217. Demonstrate aptitude for facilitating complementary healing modalities in ministry. (Source: "Standards for Certification of Chaplains," January 2001. Reproduced by permission of the National Association of Catholic Chaplains. <www.nacc.org>.)

Reflection Questions: Of the eight needed skills for spirituality discussed in Chapters 5, 6, and 7, where do you see yourself needing to grow? What skills do you see yourself as already strong in? Do you think that any significant skill has been missed? What might it be? What do you think of the various professional organizations' lists of skills of spiritual care? Are they valuable for you?

ORGANIZATIONAL STANDARDS OF SPIRITUAL CARE

We live in an exciting time for spiritual care as we see it expand outward into the larger community. Spiritual care is emerging from its traditional place in hospital chaplaincy into broader health care networks. For example, we can now find it in home care, long-term care, hospice, preventive care, support groups, and counseling centers. Spiritual care is emerging from churches and parishes to the workplace, the shopping mall, courthouses, and detention centers (Catholic Health Association of the United States, 1997). Spiritual care truly is becoming interdisciplinary as an integrating process in counseling, social systems, health care, business, and beyond.

Many of these groups want to establish solid standards of spiritual care in their organizations. However, it is not only, as in the past, a question of an organizational chart showing an employee, such as a pastoral care coordinator, whose position description focused on providing spiritual care services. Now it is more a question of how spiritual care is practically carried out throughout the whole organization's services. It is the process through which spiritual care can reach its goals. It is developing a language of spiritual care that can be used and shared among various disciplines. This requires familiarity with processes or interventions for spiritual care. It is developing an evaluation process for spiritual care (Catholic Health Association of the United States, 1990).

To accomplish this, the Joint Commission on Accreditation of Pastoral Services (JCAPS, 2000) states that organizations which provide spiritual care need to create their own "narrative description of their spiritual care services" (p. 2). This written narrative would include the goals and objectives of spiritual care together with the process steps or interventions to reach them. Moreover, another accrediting organization, the Joint Commission on the Accreditation of Health Care Organizations (JCAHO), in its new guidelines for spiritual care requires specific evidence of spiritual care, states that an accredited health care organization must show that "recognition of the spiritual needs and rights of the person are reflected in policies, procedures and administration's ability to *articulate these needs and rights*" (JCAHO, 2000, italics added). This articulation of the spiritual needs and rights of the person marvelously creates for an organization both an inventive vision for spiritual care and reliable methods to reach it. Although the goals and processes of spiritual care may appear abstract, they can be practically stated and described. This process is doubly important, as spiritual care is closely related to other areas of institutional care. Moreover, if the organizational process of spiritual care is laid out and becomes more understandable to all team members in an organization, spiritual care will be more regularly used and accepted.

Developing an Organizational Narrative Description of Spiritual Care Goals for a Spiritual Care Network

The pamphlet *Spiritual Care in a Community or Network Setting* (Catholic Health Association of the United States, 1997), lists some central goals for an organization to provide spiritual care:

- To be available and accessible to all served within the continuum of care, especially those whose illness represents a spiritual crisis

- To assess the spiritual needs of the patient within the continuum of care in light of available community resources
- To develop goals and objectives, personnel, and specific services to meet the Center's needs
- To advocate for the care and treatment of the whole person
- To empower individuals to understand the relationship between spiritual and physical well-being
- To provide appropriate prayer, sacramental, and worship opportunities
- To facilitate needed support groups
- To offer follow-up through community resources or through the Center's staff (From The Catholic Health Association, *Spiritual Care in a Community Setting,* p. 5. Copyright ©1997 by the Catholic Health Association. Reproduced with permission.)

Could you use some of these goals as your own organization's goals and to develop your own narrative of the process of spiritual care?

Spiritual Care Standards Related to Key Spiritual Needs

Every spiritual care organization needs to develop the ability to carry out an effective spiritual assessment of its helpees' spiritual needs. In Chapter 2, I described how the spiritual caregiver can determine the spiritual needs of the helpee through a listening conversation. Working with these spiritual needs can lead to desirable outcomes of acquiring the spiritual energy needed by helpees in their struggles, pains, and challenges.

The goals of spiritual care are carried out in real-life situations within human caring relationships. These goals are specifically reached through serving the spiritual needs of helpees. The following model includes standards of spiritual care that focus on the core spiritual needs of every person. (Model adapted from Topper, 1997.) An organization can have its professional helpers use any or all of the following standards when working with helpees' spirituality.

Standard one: Work with the meaning system or beliefs of helpees.

The helper will use helpees' beliefs and life meanings in the healing process. In any sickness and/or serious problem, people frequently question or doubt the core beliefs and meanings that hold their lives together. They need support in this area.

The Process. The helper will ascertain with helpees their sense of direction and meaning in life. As discussed earlier, the helper can facilitate this process through asking open-ended questions such as, "Who or what gives you strength at this time?" or "Where do you turn in times of difficulty?"

Desirable Outcome. Helpees will be able to use their sense of meaning for emotional and spiritual support.

Standard two: Work with the image of God or Higher Power of helpees.

The helper will assess the helpees' images of God or Higher Power in order to use it in the healing process. Patients may exhibit fear and guilty feelings.

The Process. The helper will ascertain whether helpees believe in a Higher Power, and if this relationship is a source of support and guidance or of punishment and retribution. The helper could ask open-ended questions such as, "I am wondering whether you believe in God, and if so what might God be saying to you in this situation?" or "What is your sense of a Higher Power or what is your spirituality?" If the helpee has a harsh image of God, the helpee might ask if he or she could ever remember another image of God.

Desirable Outcome. Helpees will grow in a healthier image of God who sustains and cares rather than an always-demanding angry God who is out to get them. They will exhibit less fear and guilt and face their sickness or problems with more hope and energy.

Standard three: Use as appropriate the spiritual/religious practices of helpees.

The helper will facilitate helpees' use of their spiritual/religious practices and resources, if desired. Helpees need to use what is familiar to them in their internal healing process.

The Process. The spiritual caregiver will ascertain whether helpees wish to use any spiritual or religious resources or practices in their care. This will be determined through the use of open-ended questions such as, "Are there any spiritual/religious practices or rituals that are important to you and how can I help you with them?" or "What spiritual/religious books, symbols, or prayers are important to you?" The helper will refer to other spiritual/religious professionals as needed.

Desirable Outcome. The helpee will receive support from the spiritual/religious resources of his or her tradition, if desired.

Standard four: Facilitate emotional and spiritual support for helpees from others around them.

Some helpees turn inward in times of pain and fear. Yet they may fear being separated from others through their sickness and even death. The helper will encourage and facilitate when possible helpees' openness to receive emotional and spiritual support from others.

The Process. The helper will ascertain whether helpees are connected with others outside themselves. Are they receiving care, love, emotional, or spiritual support from family, friends, and community? Helpers will offer their own care and spiritual support to the helpee and show and encourage helpees to look for support from others. To facilitate this, helpers may ask open-ended questions such as, "Who is or are the most important people to you?" "Are they available to you at this time?" or "What groups, churches, or communities do you belong to?"

Desirable Outcome. Helpees will experience the support and accompaniment of the helper. They will also look to others outside of themselves to receive care and support.

Standard five: Encourage helpees to care about and reach out to others. ·

Helpees, even in pain and struggle, still have the need to relate to and care for others. The helper will encourage and facilitate when possible the helpee's ability to relate to and to give love to others.

The Process. To ascertain this need to love others, the helper may ask open-ended questions such as, "What concerns or worries you the most at this time?" or "Does your present situation or condition keep you at this time from relating to those around you?"

Desirable Outcome. Helpees will connect with those around them.

Standard six: Work with any fears, guilt, etc. that helpees may experience.

In facing pain and problems, helpees frequently feel deep loss, sadness, and even despair. They may need to experience forgiveness for something in their past. The helper will facilitate helpees developing a sense of hope, forgiveness, and creativity.

The Process. The helper will ascertain whether helpees are experiencing strong fear and guilt. To do this, the helper may ask open-ended questions such as, "Is anything especially fearful for you at this time?" "Are you anxious or do you need at this time to be reconciled with anyone?" or "How do you experience forgiveness in your life?"

Desirable Outcome. Helpees will receive help with any anxieties or guilt that may hinder their feeling of peace and well-being. They will develop a better sense of hope in their situation. In this way they will develop improved physical, mental, and spiritual well-being.

A Typical Spiritual Care Model of Intervention

In general helping situations such as counseling sessions or pastoral/spiritual visits dealing with the developmental problems of life, the helper would carry out some or all of the following:

- Be an active listener.
- Develop a helping relationship. (Chapter 5)
- Identify the issue, concern, or problem.
- Address the focus of care needed whether social, emotional, spiritual, or ritual. (Chapters 2 and 3)
- Assess spiritual needs. (Chapter 2)
- Reframe the problem from a spiritual perspective and facilitate the helpee reframing it in this perspective drawing upon his or her spiritual resources. (Chapter 2)
- Determine the end goal of the spiritual care whether healing, sustaining, guiding, or reconciling and the strategies to reach this goal. (Chapter 3)
- Relate spiritual care to the helpee's religion/beliefs if needed and desired on the helpee's part. (Chapter 3)

Spiritual Care Standards with Process Steps for Specific Interventions

An organization's spiritual care will vary based on the particular concern and life situations of its helpees. Spiritual care is usually issue-focused and will be different in crisis grief and loss situations from that of general counseling sessions or home visits. What is called for in all situations is to bring spiritual awareness into the concern or problem through standards related to the specific issue.

Standards for Grief Ministry

Ryan (1997) lists the following spiritual care standards in grief ministry:

- Chaplains are available to provide pastoral grief ministry appropriate to the age of the persons served and their cultural/religious/spiritual background.
- Chaplains recognize that the ministry most required is that of compassionate presence.
- Chaplains recognize there are no "magical words" which will dispel the grief; they are at ease with the sense of powerlessness often experienced in grief ministry.
- Chaplains recognize the importance of being in touch with their own grief feelings and experiences and how they may influence their ministry here and now.
- Chaplains are at ease with the "silence" which is a necessary part of grief ministry.
- Chaplains draw upon the resources of other interdisciplinary grief members.
- Chaplains refer when help beyond their capabilities is required. (Source: Ryan, S. (1997). "Demonstrating competent spiritual care." *Vision* 7(6) June, p. 11. Reproduced by permission of the National Association of Catholic Chaplains. <www.nacc.org>.)

Standards for Childhood Survivors of Sexual Abuse

Spiritual Issues

- Counselors/chaplains may find a loss of faith and belief in a Higher Power or a very undeveloped concept of God.
- There may well be a profound sense of spiritual alienation and emptiness. "Where was God? Why did He not rescue me?"
- There may be a profound loss of hope.
- They cannot feel peace, cannot pray, and often lack direction in life.
- There are issues of anger, guilt, and shame.
- It appears that the energy, creative force, and general power that many associate with spirituality is often blocked in the life of the traumatized client. (McBride and Armstrong, 1995)

Spiritual Care Responses

- Counselors/chaplains need to allow clients to tell their stories. It is imperative that counselors communicate a sense of being loved by God and that clients are not responsible for what happened to them as a child.
- Counselors/chaplains give permission to clients to be angry, especially with God. Be nonjudgmental in allowing clients to explore spiritual issues. Counselors expressing unconditional acceptance may be survivors' only experience that demonstrates the possibility of God being able to love them in the same way.
- Counselors/chaplains help clients recognize that forgiveness is not simply an act but a process that can be begun and completed only after working through the issues concerned and their accompanying feelings. Do not try to rush this process by questioning their pace or suggesting forgiveness as the first step.
- It is recommended that counselors use every avenue to give clients reassurance of their acceptability before God and their place in God's plan.
- When appropriate, counselors/chaplains celebrate, bless, and praise survivors' rediscovery of a God of hope, a God of great comfort, and a God of great respect for them. (McBride and Armstrong, 1995)

As the field of spiritual care grows and evolves, many more processes of spiritual treatment for many specific concerns and problems will evolve with it. For example, St. Joseph Medical Center in Tacoma, Washington, lists several issues, such as difficulty coping with cancer, onset of new disability, pervasive anger, self-destructive lifestyle, and major change in body image, that spiritual care could respond to with specific interventions (Hilsman, 1997).

Accrediting bodies for health care and other community agencies are calling for and making requirements for quality spiritual care. It is no longer sufficient only to have someone working under that title. Spiritual care is becoming part of the whole organization's focus on whole-person health. This section on organizational standards of spiritual care identified and explained some key considerations and questions around spiritual care for organizational development. This is only the beginning of a marvelous process of integrating spirituality more fully into human services.

Reflection Questions: Do you think there can be organizational guidelines or structures to facilitate spiritual care as part of whole-person care? If so, how might your organization establish helping standards of spiritual care? What do you see as the main standards of spiritual care needed in a helping organization? What standards of spiritual care are valuable for work with the specific spiritual issues of your helpees?

References

Preface

Burke, M. (2000). From the chair. *CACREP Connection,* Winter, p. 2. (Available from the Center for the Accreditation of Counseling Programs, <www.counseling.org/cacrep>.)

Carpenito, L. (1997). *Nursing diagnosis,* Seventh Edition. New York: Lippincott.

Clinebell, H. (1984). *Basic types of pastoral care and counseling,* Revised and Enlarged Edition. Nashville: Abingdon Press.

Giblin, P. and Stark-Dykema, J. (1992). Master's level pastoral counseling training. *Journal of Pastoral Care, 46* (4), 362-371.

Koenig, H. (1997). *Is religion good for your health?: The effects of religion on physical and mental health.* Binghamton, NY: The Haworth Press.

McSherry, E. (1987). Ongoing clinical research in the spiritual dimension of health specialist practitioners. *Care Giver Journal, 4* (1), 30-32.

Pruyser, P. (1976). *The minister as diagnostician.* Philadelphia: The Westminster Press.

Report to members from the leadership boards of ACPE (The Association of Clinical Pastoral Education), NACC (The National Association of Catholic Chaplains), and APC (The Association of Professional Chaplains) (2001). *Vision, 2* (3), 5-9. (Available from The National Association of Catholic Chaplains, <www.nacc.org>.)

Chapter 1

Allport, G. (1968). *The person in psychology: Selected essays.* Boston: Beacon Press.

American Psychiatric Association (1994). *Diagnostic and statistical manual of mental disorders,* Fourth Edition. Washington, DC: American Psychiatric Association.

Carpenito, L. (1997). *Nursing diagnosis,* Seventh Edition. New York: Lippincott.

Clinebell, H. (1966). *Basic types of pastoral counseling,* First Edition. Nashville: Abingdon Press.

Clinebell, H. (1995). *Counseling for spiritually empowered wholeness.* Binghamton, NY: The Haworth Press.

Colliton, M. (1981). The spiritual dimension of nursing. In I. Beland and J. Passos (Eds.), *Clinical nursing* (pp. 492-499). New York: Macmillan Publishing Co.

Faiver, C., Ingersoll, R. E., O'Brien, E., and McNally, C. (2001). *Explorations in counseling and spirituality.* Belmont, CA: Brooks/Cole.

Fish, S. and Shelly, J. (1983). *Spiritual care,* Second Edition. Downers Grove, IL: InterVarsity Press.

Fitchett, G. (1993). *Assessing spiritual needs: A guide for caregivers.* Minneapolis: Augsburg.

Helminiak, D. (1996). *The human core of spirituality.* Albany, NY: State University of New York Press.

Highfield, M. and Cason, C. (1983). Spiritual needs of patients: Are they recognized? *Cancer Nursing,* June, 187-192.

Ivy, S. (1988). Pastoral diagnosis as pastoral caring. *Journal of Pastoral Care, 42* (1), 81-89.

Jung, C. (1959). On the nature of the psyche. In V. de Laszlo (Ed.), *The basic writings of C. G. Jung* (pp. 37-104). New York: Random House (Modern Library Series).

Kelly, E. (1995). *Spirituality and religion in counseling and psychotherapy.* Alexandria, VA: American Counseling Association.

Kim, Mi Ja, McFarland, G., and McLane, A. (1995). *Pocket guide to nursing diagnoses,* Sixth Edition. St. Louis: Mosby.

Kuhn, C. (1998). A spiritual inventory of the medically ill patient. *Psychiatric Medicine, 6* (2), 87-100.

Loury, R. J. (Ed.) (1979). *The journals of Abraham Maslow,* 2 vols. Monterey, CA: Brooks/Cole.

Lowen, A. (1990). *The spirituality of the body.* New York: Macmillan Publishing Co.

May, R. (1989). *The art of counseling.* New York: Gardner Press.

McBrien, R. (1987). *Ministry: A theological, pastoral handbook.* San Francisco: Harper and Row.

Moberg, D. (1971). *Spiritual well-being: Background and issues.* Washington, DC: The White House Conference on Aging.

Moore, D. and Saad, L. (1999). CNN/USA Today/Gallup Poll. Princeton, NJ: The Gallup Organization, December 9-12.

O'Brien, M. (1982). The need for spiritual integrity. In H. Yura and M. Walsh (Eds.), *Human needs and the nursing process* (pp. 85-115). Norwalk, CT: Appleton-Century-Crofts.

Peterson, E. (1985). The physical, the spiritual. Can you meet all of your patients' needs? *Journal of Gerontological Nursing, 11* (10), 23-27.

Prozesky, M. (1984). *Religion and ultimate well-being: An explanatory theory.* New York: St. Martin's Press.

Thayer, N. (1985). *Spirituality and pastoral care.* Philadelphia: Fortress Press.

Van Kaam, A. (1975). *In search of spiritual identity.* Denville, NJ: Dimension Books.

Chapter 2

American Psychiatric Association (1994). *Diagnostic and statistical manual of mental disorders,* Fourth Edition. Washington, DC: American Psychiatric Association.

Bergin, A. (1988). Three contributions of a spiritual perspective to psychotherapy and behavior change. In W. Martin and J. Martin (Eds.), *Behavior therapy and religion* (pp. 25-36). Newbury Park, NY: Sage Publications.

Dossey, B. (1998). Holistic modalities and healing moments. *American Journal of Nursing, 98* (6), 44-47.

Fitchett, G. (1993). *Assessing spiritual needs: A guide for caregivers.* Minneapolis: Augsburg.

Fitchett, G. (1995). Linda Krauss and the lap of God. *Second Opinion, 20* (4), 41-50.

Ivy, S. (1987). A faith development/self-development model for pastoral assessment. *The Journal of Pastoral Care, 41* (4), 329-340.

Malony, H. (1996). How counselors can help people become more spiritual through religious assessment. In H. Grzymala-Moszczynska and B. Beit-Hallahmi (Eds.), *Religion, psychopathology, and coping* (pp. 245-259). Atlanta, GA: Rodopi.

Nash, R. (1990). Life's major spiritual issues: An emerging framework for spiritual assessment and diagnosis. *The Care Giver Journal, 7* (1), 3-42.

Oates, W. (1982). *The Christian pastor,* Third Edition, Revised. Philadelphia: The Westminster Press.

Stoll, R. (1979). Guidelines for spiritual assessment. *American Journal of Nursing,* September, 1574-1577.

Topper, C. (1996). Intentional spiritual assessment: A self assessment model. *Vision: The National Association of Catholic Chaplains, 6* (3), 21.

Chapter 3

Clebsch, W. and Jaekle, C. (1964). *Pastoral care in historical perspective.* Englewood Cliffs, NJ: Prentice-Hall, Inc.

Ellwood, R. (1990). Religion. In R. J. Hunter (Ed.), *Dictionary of pastoral care and counseling* (p. 1054). Nashville: Abingdon Press.

Kelly, E. (1995). Assessing the spiritual dimension in counseling. In E. Kelly (Ed.), *Spirituality and religion in counseling and psychotherapy* (pp. 131-187). Alexandria, VA: The American Counseling Association.

Malony, H. (1988). The clinical assessment of optimal religious functioning. *Review of Religious Research, 30* (1), 3-17.

Malony, H. (1996). How counselors can help people become more spiritual through religious assessment. In H. Grzymala-Moszczynska and B. Beit-Hallahmi (Eds.), *Religion, psychopathology, and coping* (pp. 245-259). Atlanta, GA: Rodopi.

Malony, N. (1994). The uses of religious assessment in counseling. In L. Brown (Ed.), *Religion, personality, and mental health.* New York: Springer-Verlag.

Norris, K. (1998). *Amazing grace: A vocabulary of faith.* New York: Riverhead Books.

Oates, W. (1982). *The Christian pastor,* Third Edition, Revised. Philadelphia: The Westminster Press.

Patton, J. (1985). The new language of pastoral counseling. In G. L. Borchert and A. D. Lester (Eds.), *Spiritual dimensions of pastoral care* (pp. 72-89). Philadelphia: The Westminster Press.

Princeton Religious Research Center (1993). *Religion in America, 1992-1993.* Princeton, NJ: Princeton Religious Research Center.

Pruyser, P. (1976). *The minister as diagnostician.* Philadelphia: The Westminster Press.

Sackett, G. (1985). Seven dimensions of spirituality. *The Care Giver Journal, 1* (2), 27-30.

Chapter 4

Arnold, S. D. (1996). Spiritual care guides: Common language the key. *Vision, 6,* (3), 12-15.

Capps, D. (1979). *Pastoral care: A thematic approach.* Philadelphia: The Westminster Press.

Catholic Health Association of the United States. (1990). *Quality assurance and pastoral care.* St. Louis: The Catholic Health Association.

Ellison, C. W. (1983). Spiritual well-being: Conceptualization and measurement. *Journal of Psychology and Spirituality, 11* (4), 330-340.

Farran, C., Fitchett, G., Quiring-Emblem, J., and Burck, J. (1989). Development of a model for spiritual assessment and intervention. *Journal of Religion and Health, 26* (3), 185-194.

Fitchett, G. (1993). *Assessing spiritual needs.* Minneapolis: Augsburg.

Fowler, J. (1981). *Stages of faith: The psychology of human development and the quest for meaning.* San Francisco: Harper.

Fowler, J. (1990). Faith development research. In R. J. Hunter (Ed.), *Dictionary of pastoral care and counseling* (pp. 399-401). Nashville: Abingdon Press.

Genia, V. (1991). The spiritual experience index: A measure of spiritual maturity. *Journal of Religion and Health, 30* (4), 337-347.

Genia, V. (1997). The spiritual experience index: Revision and reformulation. *Review of Religious Research, 38* (4), 344-361.

Hay, M. (1989). Principles of building spiritual assessment tools. *The American Journal of Hospice Care,* September/October, 25-31.

Ivy, S. (1987). A faith development/self-development model for pastoral assessment. *The Journal of Pastoral Care, 41* (4), 329-340.

Kass, J., Friedman, R., Leserman, J., Zuttermeister, P., and Benson, H. (1991). Health outcomes and a new index of spiritual experience. *Journal for the Scientific Study of Religion, 30,* 203-211.

Kelly, E. (1995). Assessing the spiritual/religious dimension in counseling. In E. Kelly (Ed.), *Spirituality and religion in counseling and psychotherapy* (pp. 131-187). Alexandria, VA: American Counseling Association.

McSherry, E. (1987a). Economic impact of chaplaincy on the hospital environment. *The CareGiver Journal, 4* (1), 29-41.

McSherry, E. (1987b). Modernization of the clinical science of chaplaincy. *The CareGiver Journal, 4* (1), 1-13.

McSherry, E. (1987c). The spiritual assessment profile, Brockton/West Roxbury VAMC (125), 1400 VFW Parkway, West Roxbury, MA 02132; 617-323-7700.

National Interfaith Coalition on Aging (1975). *Spiritual well-being: A definition.* Athens, GA: NICA.

Paloutzian, R. and Ellison, C. (1982). Loneliness, spiritual well-being and the quality of life. In L. A. Peplau and D. Perlman (Eds.), *Loneliness: A sourcebook of current theory, research and therapy* (pp. 224-237). New York: Wiley.

Paloutzian, R. and Ellison, C. (1991). *Manual for the spiritual well-being scale.* Nyack, NY: Life Advances.

Richards, P. and Bergin, A. (1997). *A spiritual strategy for counseling and psychotherapy.* Washington, DC: American Psychological Association.

Stoddard, G. and Burns-Haney, J. (1990). Developing an integrated approach to spiritual assessment: One department's experience. *The CareGiver Journal, 7* (4), 63-86.

VandeCreek, L. (Ed.) (1995). *Spiritual needs and pastoral services: Reading in research.* Decatur, GA: Journal of Pastoral Care Publications.

VandeCreek, L., Ayres, S., and Bassham, M. (1995). Using INSPIRIT to conduct spiritual assessments. *Journal of Pastoral Care, 49* (4), 83-89.

Veach, T. and Chappel, J. (1992). Measuring spiritual health. *Substance Abuse, 13* (3), 139-147.

Chapter 5

Bonhoeffer, D. (1985). *Spiritual Care.* Philadelphia, PA: Fortress Press.

Burns, D. (1980). *Feeling good: The new mood therapy.* New York: Signet Books.

Cameron, J. (1998). *The right to write.* New York: Penguin Putnam.

Campbell, A. (1981). *Rediscovering pastoral care.* Philadelphia: The Westminster Press.

Clinebell, H. (1984). *Basic types of pastoral care and counseling,* Revised and Enlarged Edition. Nashville: Abingdon Press.

Combs, A. (1989). *A theory of therapy: Guidelines for counseling practice.* Newbury Park, CA: Sage Publications.

Dittes, J. (1990). Analytic (Jungian) psychology and theology. In R. J. Hunter (Ed.), *Dictionary of pastoral care and counseling* (pp. 29-33). Nashville: Abingdon Press.

Goldsmith, J. (1986). *Practicing the presence.* San Francisco: Harper.

May, R. (1989). *The art of counseling,* Revised Edition. New York: Gardner Press.

Pew-Fetzer Task Force (1994). *Relationship-centered care.* San Francisco: Pew Health Professions Commission.

Rogers, C. (1958). The characteristics of a helping relationship. *Personnel and Guidance Journal, 37,* 6-16.

Rogers, C. (1961). *On becoming a person.* Boston: Houghton Mifflin.

Traupman, R. (2000). A maturing presbyterate. *For Priests Only, V* (6), 1.

Williams, E. and Williams, E. (1992). *Spiritually aware pastoral care.* Mahwah, NJ: Paulist Press.

Chapter 6

Al-Tantawi, S. A. (1997). *General introduction to Islam,* Second Edition. Jeddah, Saudi Arabia: Al-Manara Publishing.

Altareb, B. (1996). Islamic spirituality in America: A middle path to unity. *Counseling and Values, 41,* 29-38.

Association for Clinical Pastoral Education, Inc. (2001). *The standards of the association for clinical pastoral education.* Decator, GA: Association for Clinical Pastoral Education, Inc.

Carpenito, L. (1997). *Nursing diagnosis,* Seventh Edition. New York: Lippincott.

Faiver, C., Ingersoll, R., O'Brien, E., and McNally, C. (2001). *Explorations in counseling and spirituality.* Belmont, CA: Brooks/Cole.

George, M. (2000). *Discover inner peace: A guide to spiritual well-being.* San Francisco: Chronicle Books.

Green, J. (1999). *Cultural awareness in the human services: A multi-ethnic approach,* Third Edition. Boston: Allyn and Bacon.

Grollman, E. A. (1990). Jewish care and counseling. In R. J. Hunter (Ed.), *Dictionary of pastoral care and counseling* (pp. 601-606). Nashville: Abingdon Press.

Jacobi, J. and Hull, R. F. C. (1970). *C. G. Jung: Psychological reflections, A new anthology of his writings.* Princeton, NJ: Princeton University Press.

Jensen, J. P. and Bergin, A. E. (1988). Mental health values of professional therapists: A national interdisciplinary survey. *Professional Psychology: Research and Practice, 19,* 290-297.

Jung, C. (1961). *Psychology and religion.* Princeton: Princeton University Press.

Kelly, E. W. (1995). *Spirituality and religion in counseling and psychotherapy.* Alexandria, VA: American Counseling Association.

Kenny, D. (June, 1980). Clinical pastoral education: Exploring covenants with God. *Journal of Pastoral Care, 34* (2), 152-155.

Koenig, H. G. (1997). *Is religion good for your health?: The effects of religion on physical and mental health.* Binghamton, NY: The Haworth Press.

Koenig, H. G. (1999). *The healing power of faith: Science explores medicine's last great frontier.* New York: Simon and Schuster.

Koenig, H. G., McCullough, M. E., and Larson, D. B. (2001). *Handbook of religion and health.* New York: Oxford University Press.

Larson, D. and Larson, S. (1991). Religious commitment and health: Valuing the relationship. *Second Opinion: Health, Faith, and Ethics, 17* (1), 26-40.

Larson, D. and Larson, S. (1994). *The forgotten factor in physical and mental health: What does the research say?* Chicago, IL: The Templeton Foundation Press.

McGoldrick, M., Pearce, J., and Giordano, J. (Eds.) (1982). *Ethnicity and family therapy.* New York: Guilford Press.

Norris, K. (1998). *Amazing grace: A vocabulary of faith.* New York: Riverhead Books.

Princeton Religious Research Center (1993). *Religion in America, 1992-1993.* Princeton, NJ: Princeton Religious Research Center.

Propst, L., Ostrom, R., Watkins, P., Dean, T., and Mashburn, D. (1992). Comparative efficacy of religious and nonreligious cognitive-behavioral therapy for the treatment of clinical depression in religious individuals. *Journal of Consulting and Clinical Psychology, 60* (1), 94-103.

Pruyser, P. (1976). *The minister as diagnostician.* Philadelphia: The Westminster Press.

Richards, P. S. and Bergin, A. E. (1997). *A spiritual strategy for counseling and psychotherapy.* Washington, DC: American Psychological Association.

Rogers, C. (1942). *Counseling and psychotherapy.* Boston: Houghton Mifflin.

Smith, H. (1991). *The world's religions.* San Francisco: Harper.

Teasdale, W. (1999). *The mystic heart: Discovering a universal spirituality in the world's religions.* Novato, CA: New World Library.

Willimon, W. H. (1979). *Worship as pastoral care.* Nashville: Abingdon Press.

Chapter 7

Association of Professional Chaplains. "About APC, mission/vision/values." <http://www.professionalchaplains.org/index1.html>. November 20, 2002, p.1.

Benjamin, P. and Looby, J. (1998). Defining the nature of spirituality in the context of Maslow's and Rogers' theories. *Counseling and Values, 41,* 29-38.

Burke, M. (2000). From the chair. *CACREP Connection,* Winter, p. 2. (Available from the Center for the Accreditation of Counseling Programs, <www.counseling.org/cacrep>.)

Catholic Health Association of the United States (1990). *Quality assurance and pastoral care.* St. Louis: The Catholic Health Association.

Catholic Health Association of the United States (1997). *Spiritual care in a community or network setting.* St. Louis: The Catholic Health Association.

Council for Accreditation of Counseling and Related Educational Programs (CACREP). "The 2001 standards." <http://www.counseling.org/cacrep>. November 30, 2002, pp. 1-41.

Doran, J. (1984). *Spirituality and justice.* Maryknoll, NY: Orbis Books.

Hilsman, G. (1997). Spiritual pathways: One response to the current standards challenge. *Vision, 7* (6), 8-9.

International Pastoral Care Network for Social Responsibility. <http://www.ipcnsr. org>. November 30, 2002.

Joint Commission on Accreditation of Health Care Organizations (JCAHO) 2000. New JCAHO guidelines for spiritual care. <http://www.professionalchaplains. org/resources/jcahoguide.html>. November 30, pp. 1-5.

Joint Commission on Accreditation of Pastoral Services (JCAPS) 2000. Accreditation process summary. <http://www.comissnetwork.org/jcaps>. August 14, pp. 1-5.

Lewis, J., Lewis, M., Daniels, J., D'Andrea, M. (1998). *Community counseling: Empowerment strategies for a diverse society,* Second Edition. Boston: Brooks/ Cole.

Maslow, A. (1968). *Toward a psychology of being.* Princeton: Van Nostrand.

McBride, J. and Armstrong, G. (1995). The spiritual components of chronic post traumatic stress disorder. *Journal of Religion and Health, 34* (1), 5-16.

National Association of Catholic Chaplains (2001). "Standards for certification of chaplains," Section 400. <http://www.nacc.org>. November 30, 2002, pp. 1-3.

National Conference of Catholic Bishops (1979). Brothers and sisters to us: U.S. bishops' pastoral letter on racism in our day. Washington, DC: National Conference of Catholic Bishops.

Ryan, S. (1997). Demonstrating competent spiritual care. *Vision, 7* (6), 10-12.

Thomas: Legislative information on the Internet. <http://thomas.loc.gov>. November 30, 2002.

Topper, C. (1997). A model for developing standards. *Vision, 7* (6), 9-10.